The Dramatic Impulse
in Modern Poetics

The Dramatic Impulse in Modern Poetics

DON GEIGER

LOUISIANA STATE UNIVERSITY PRESS
BATON ROUGE

*To Francine Merritt and Wolcott Ely,
with affection and esteem*

Copyright © 1967 by
Louisiana State University Press

Library of Congress Catalog Card Number: 67–26972
Manufactured in the United States of America by
Thos. J. Moran's Sons, Inc.
Designed by Jules B. McKee

PREFACE

*P*ERHAPS the appropriate point of entry into this book is marked by Chester Long's recent conclusion, following his canvass of writings in oral interpretation studies, that "nothing inclusive enough has been written by scholars in our field on the ontology of the poem." [1] Professor Long's study confirms my mere impression. And, after Long has joined me in knowing what I have written in the following papers, both of us will continue to think his conclusion correct. Thus I begin with "perhaps." But "perhaps" is a good word to use when questioning ontology, which is a desperate plunge—as Lucifer was first to discover to his grief. In calling for study of "the nature of poetic texts" and "the text and its relation to the poem and to performance," [2] Long not only indicates proper headings for the thorough essay on ontology for which we wait but also points the general direction of matters discussed herein. Consequently, although my essay will not settle our various problems affecting ontology (I lean again on Long, supposing with him that we are a pleasant distance from "absolutely final conclusions" about, probably, *any* aspect of theory [3]), I can hope to stir up a few questions in

[1] Chester C. Long, "The Poem's Text as a Technique of Performance in Public Group Readings of Poetry," *Western Speech,* XXXI (Winter, 1967), 17.

[2] *Ibid.,* 18.

[3] *Ibid.,* 29.

an area of oral interpretation studies in which "literary" and "speech" concerns merge.

Some part of the area to be surveyed is, I think, the domain of the poem's dramatic speaker. The notion of the dramatic speaker is a particularly modern one, but a certain curiosity attaches to its treatment in modern criticism. Students of poetry by and large refer as a matter of course to the poem's speaker. Yet it has been suggested that the dramatic speaker inhabits a theoretic no-man's-land. Monroe Beardsley reports that "the concept of the dramatic speaker—'persona,' 'mask'— is widely used in criticism but seldom analyzed." [4] A characteristic critical reliance on the concept, however, suggests that, far from being a chance piece of analytic apparatus, it is deeply involved in major concerns of contemporary poetics. This is the likelihood which claims my attention in these papers.

Most of what follows was delivered first at the thirty-second annual Conference on Speech Education at Louisiana State University. That I assumed an audience of persons having a day to pull themselves together between lectures will be readily apparent to the enduring reader. Hence, I will not elaborate the effect of the occasion on the content of these papers; they will have their own say regardless of what I say about them. But for a quite different reason I can say little more of my sense of the conference itself. I cannot hope to convey my pleasure and, indeed, delight in its proceedings. At the beginning of the conference I greeted respected colleagues and students, both graduate and undergraduate, of whom I had prior reason to think well. At its conclusion, I departed with a treasure in memories of their courtesy and kindness in stimulating comradeship. These are the gifts of friends, and by their friends remembered. In completing this work I have

---

[4] Monroe C. Beardsley, *Aesthetics: Problems in the Philosophy of Criticism* (New York and Burlingame, Calif.: Harcourt, Brace and World, 1958) , 260.

been significantly aided by Katharine Hershey, editor, and Richard Wentworth, director, of the Louisiana State University Press, and also by editorial readers whose names are unknown to me. With gratitude I thank these persons as I have privately thanked still other persons whose generous assistance and encouragement sustained me in bringing these lectures to print.

D. G.

Berkeley, California

CONTENTS

*The Dramatic Impulse
in Modern Poetics*

Toward a Poetics
for Making,
Seeing, and Saying

$\mathcal{I}$N this book I shall discuss some aspects of poetry—particularly the species termed variously the "lyric" or "short" or "I" poem—as dramatized speech or utterance. My viewpoint is combative only in its amiable if not merely innocuous assumption that significant problems in theory of poetry and its analysis remain unsolved. Although dramatic theory, as one of several perspectives in poetics, doubtless has distant relations which I cannot see, it has nearer ones which I can; hence I should state my understanding of these relations.

The view offered here, though richly funded by the New Criticism, is a theoretic alternative—though by way of inclusion rather than contradiction—to contextualist theory, which also derives from New Criticism. In some measure contextualism refers to an attitude more or less cloudily in the atmosphere of contemporary critical practice rather than to a doctrine. But Murray Krieger has given the attitude theoretic articulation. Variously equating it with New Criticism[1] and identifying it as the "residual first principle of the New Criticism," Krieger summarizes contextualism thus: "It holds that each literary work must, as literature and not another thing, strive to become a self-sufficient system of symbols that comes to terms with itself." [2]

[1] Murray Krieger, "After the New Criticism," *Massachusetts Review*, IV (Autumn, 1962), 184.
[2] *Ibid.*, 187. I do not cite Krieger's summation casually. As he notes

Treatment of a poem as a "self-sufficient system" or as language "coming to terms with itself" delivers the poem, as Louise Rosenblatt reports in some dismay, as "an object, like a machine." [3] In the climate of opinion created by contextualism, suggestions that "the modern lyric is autonomous, a separate mobile, having its own private design and performance" [4] or that a poem is best thought of "as a 'box to be opened,' a created object, a Japanese garden—not a message or confession" [5] may seem to be truisms. But, far from being truisms to the theorist, they but point to the considerable sacrifice incurred by contextualism when its theoretic implications are exclusively pursued. Thus emphasized, contextualism implies some massive indifferences: to the audience (the poem is not a message), to the poet's impulse to express his way of looking at things (the poem is not a confession), and to the representation of life or raw experience (the poem is a "separate mobile").

Like Krieger (and many others), I think contextualism an insufficient poetics;[6] unlike Krieger, I do not think that New

---

in his essay, Krieger bases his conclusion on an exhaustive study—remarkable for its honest care and patience in attending the New Criticism as a serious influence in theory of poetry—in *The New Apologists for Poetry.* (Minneapolis: University of Minnesota Press, 1956). Thus Krieger's identification of New Criticism as, in theoretic perspective, contextualism carries one line of analysis to what may approximate an official conclusion.

[3] Louise M. Rosenblatt, "The Poem as Event," *College English,* XXVI (November, 1964), 127.

[4] May Swenson, "Essay," in Symposium on Richard Wilbur, *Berkeley Review 3* (1958), 42.

[5] Richard Wilbur, "Commentary," *Berkeley Review 3* (1958), 49. It should be emphasized that both Miss Swenson and Wilbur offer their statements not as theories but as truisms—that is, as casual remarks of the sort a poet (or critic) may make in a context which does not challenge his close consideration of theoretic implications.

[6] In calling attention to differences between Krieger's and my views of the New Criticism, I should also like to stress a central similarity in attitude. While describing the New Criticism as a "lately departed" and "even exhausted" movement, Krieger urges that "the most promising critical avenues" in current literary theory are "probably those pursued in full and sympathetic awareness of those already explored" in New

Criticism reduces to contextualist theory. But contextualism surely derives from a theoretic ambivalence—if not an outright internal division—in the development of New Criticism. The New Critical movement began in a determined attack on one kind of theory of poetry as a mode of utterance. That was, as we well know, the Romantic kind, according to which the poem is its author's utterance of emotion. Much of what I have to say consists in examining the actual character, as I understand it, of the modern or New Critical response to Romantic doctrine. But to consider the matter hypothetically for the moment, if one wishes to challenge a given theory of poetry as a mode of utterance, one line of attack would be simply to deny that a poem is an utterance. Contextualism, as Krieger summarizes it, assumes that the New Criticism—in its emphasis on the poet as a maker and the poem as a total or structure of meaning—represents this denial. To offer the poem, as a contextualist might, as "a unique and self-contained form of discourse," puts gravely in question whether a poem can in fact be thought of as discourse. As Krieger observes acutely, poetry "must be in some sense referential to be a form of discourse at all." Thus, although Krieger praises the achievements of contextualism, he finds too restrictive a line of critical thought which would seem to deliver the poem as a "closed world of meaning" which is entirely "nonreferential" in character.[7]

Given this understanding of contextualism, whatever its limitations, we may more easily understand why a contextualist theory of the poem as an object—despite its indifference to expressive, imitative, and communicative dimensions of poetry—could have exerted a considerable influence in modern poetics. Contextualism is a sufficient—and its thoroughly con-

Criticism. See Krieger, "After the New Criticism," 205. Like Krieger, I would hope that critics generally will treat this movement as a seed-bed to be cultivated rather than a patch of weeds to be destroyed.

[7] Murray Krieger, *The Tragic Vision* (New York: Holt, Rinehart and Winston, 1960), 236–37.

vinced advocate would think it a necessary—reason for believing that the words in their order in a poem cannot be altered without damage to content and meaning.

That modern readers of poetry are widely agreed in this belief is a tribute to New Critical insights, for it is not a self-evident truth. In theory of poetry as speech or utterance, the unalterability of poetic content becomes an assumption requiring analysis. We know, for example, that at least *some* kinds of utterance may be altered without damage to content. We assume that particular potentiality each time we ask a question of this sort: "Do you mean by *that* (utterance A) *this* (utterance B)?" To treat poetry as a mode of speech requires our explaining why it is not a mode to which this order of question is entirely appropriate.

Contextualism relieves us of that necessity. Obviously an object cannot be altered without altering the object. Thus, since the content of an object is the object itself, it is equally obvious that an object cannot be altered without altering its content. It only remains for contextualism, thus girded in unassailable tautologies, to prove an almost equally self-evident proposition: that alteration of the finished object which is the completed poem—whether it be in the critic's paraphrase or in the poet's statement of intended effect—represents damage or loss rather than improvement. That proposition, within contextualism's frame of reference, is a pleasure to defend. But only a thoroughly convinced contextualist—and I am not sure that he is to be found in the flesh, for, as responsible critics, we rise above the vexatious embarrassments of our theories—will think that contextualism solves rather than begs questions involving transposition of poetic content into other statements or verbal orders.

Once we observe contextualism in the aforementioned perspective, as Krieger's excellent summation permits us to, we are in a position to see that it not only sacrifices explanation of important dimensions of poetry but also a major aspect of its generative impulse in New Criticism. The actual legacy of the New Criticism is richer, even if more confusing, than the contextualist aesthetic implies. Contextualism disentangles from the New Criticism those strands of thought permitting systematic statement of the poem's status as a verbal object. But that treatment makes only more evident that other strands of New Critical analysis, excluded by contextualism, suggest that we best view the poem as a mode of speech.

Cleanth Brooks and Robert Penn Warren, in a poetry text-book widely assumed to have brought New Criticism into the classroom, offer a simple and direct illustration. "All poetry," they suggest, "involves a dramatic organization . . . every poem implies a speaker of the poem . . . the poem represents the reaction of such a person." [8] This is not an isolated remark in the New Criticism; it echoes an emphasis so pervasive that conception of the poem's speaker is, in practical effect, a fixed convention or working principle in modern analysis and elucidation of poems. But conceptions of the speaker, and of the poem as a representation of his reactions, fit so loosely as to contradict contextualism. If the poem is, as contextualism presents it, truly a *self*-sufficient system, it hardly requires the *other* self of a speaker; if a poem is truly language coming to terms with *itself*, it can hardly welcome the *other* self of a speaker into its narcissistic negotiations. Discussion of a poem as its speaker's reactions creates other expectancies.

Once we assume that each poem implies its speaker, as readers of the poem we do not expect to shoulder our way into a self-sufficient system of symbols. Instead we expect that poetry, though it be but one among a variety of modes of speech, necessarily will partake of characteristic conditions of

[8] Cleanth Brooks and Robert Penn Warren, *Understanding Poetry* (New York: Henry Holt and Company, 1938), 23.

utterance. Characteristically a speaker speaks in order to say something and because there is someone (even if he is talking only to himself) to whom he wants to say it. This view, though I leave for subsequent papers its more precise statement and implication, is, I think, basic to understanding poems as dramatized utterances.

Evidently, then, dramatic theory attends in a perspective different from that of contextualism the New Criticism's quarrel with Romantic doctrines of poetic utterance. If contextualism sifts New Criticism for evidence that the poem is not an utterance, dramatic theory treats New Criticism as a developing reinterpretation, in contrast with Romanticism, of the *kind* of utterance to be found in poetry.

One way, probably the most accurate way, of understanding this state of affairs is to acknowledge that our inheritance from the New Criticism, in part suggesting that we survey the poem as a verbal object and in part indicating that we will best attend the poem as speech or utterance, includes more than one first principle. If that is the case, as I think it is, the New Criticism's is not the first will and testament to contain some confusing clauses in the assignment of good property. Still, bequeathal of two first principles is not an *unmixed* blessing, and, in so far as the legacy makes for theoretic ambiguity, doubtless it is an embarrassment of riches. There is a perspective in which Brooks's treatment of the poem as "a little drama" is a distinguished case in point. For Brooks, as we have noted, there is a sense in which "drama" posits the poem as dramatized utterance, that is, the utterance of an implicit or fictive speaker. But again, "drama" is for Brooks an analogy revealing the poem as an object. In discussing "the importance of context" in determining the "organic" whole which is the poem, Brooks compares the poem to "a growing plant" and again to "a little drama," saying that "in a good poem, as in a good drama, there is no waste motion and no superfluous parts" [9] Heavy-handed analysis is not required to see in this analogy description of a sort appropriate to a good automatic toaster or washing machine or, in this case, an efficiently structured verbal object.

But we should not too quickly dismiss this duality in comprehending poetry's dramatic nature as merely theoretic equivocation. Brooks's dual referents of "drama" may also suggest a desire to relate insights deriving from analysis of poetry as objects to insights deriving from its analysis as utterance. W. K. Wimsatt, Jr., states it as the desire "to see the poem as both expression and artifact—and the poet as both sayer and maker." [10] Thus, I would have the poem understood as an utterance in which there is no—or at least little—"waste motion."

I point toward a pleasing time when to ask whether the poem is object or utterance will be an unreal question, when our reference to the poem as a dramatized verbal utterance or a dramatic verbal object will express the same analytic regard. Such a resolution probably does not require new theories so much as it requires squaring implications with intention in contemporary statements of the nature of poetry. We may note, for example, Krieger's finding signs in Brooks and Wimsatt of an "uncompromising, all-or nothing" defense of contextualism.[11] We have observed a certain ambivalence in Brooks's dual regard of the poem as a saying and an object, and I will not argue that nothing in Wimsatt's writings permits Krieger's interpretation. But certainly neither Brooks nor Wimsatt altogether intends contextualism as Krieger defines it. Suggesting that to regard a poem "as an object or thing" is a

[9] Cleanth Brooks, "Irony as a Principle of Structure," in John Oliver Perry (ed.), *Approaches to the Poem* (San Francisco: Chandler Publishing Co., 1965), 197.

[10] W. K. Wimsatt, Jr., *The Verbal Icon* (New York: Noonday Press, 1965), xviii.

[11] Krieger, "After the New Criticism," 185.

highly instructive analogy, Wimsatt emphasizes that it is *only* an analogy: "For if anything about poetry is clear at all it is that a poem is not really a thing, like a horse or a house, but only analogically so." The poem is not "a literal nonverbal object," Wimsatt asserts, but it is surely, "if it is anything at all, a verbal discourse." [12]

Wimsatt directs his emphasis against neo-Aristotelian or Chicago critics who would treat poetry as "a special class of made objects" [13] and who consider as fundamental to proper judgment of a work "its distinctive status as a 'poetic' object." [14] Yet the object-emphasis of the Chicago critics is less exclusive than Wimsatt assumes. As in due course we shall observe more closely, the discussion by one of these critics, Elder Olson, of a lyric poem as an object becomes analysis of the structure of a speaker's reported experience. Thus it would seem that there is a point of recognition of poetry's dramatic nature at which the critic of poetic objects, whether he be of New Critical or neo-Aristotelian persuasion, is ready to assume with Wimsatt that in poetic discourse "the only 'thing' is the poet speaking." [15]

If, as I think, this comment by Wimsatt foreshadows the ground on which we may hope to reconcile theories of poetry as artifact and as utterance, we may well consider with fresh fascination how weighted with implication, and how perilous, are our theoretic descriptions of the relation of the poet to his poem. Were we to shear Wimsatt's foregoing remark from other of his comments and from general contemporary literary thought, we might reasonably think it a laconic restatement of Coleridge's famous conclusion: "What is poetry? is so nearly the same question with, What is a poet? that the answer to the one is involved in the solution to the other. For it is a

---

12 Wimsatt, *The Verbal Icon*, 50.
13 R. S. Crane (ed.), *Critics and Criticism* (Chicago: University of Chicago Press, 1952), 13.
14 *Ibid.*, 15.
15 Wimsatt, *The Verbal Icon*, 50.

distinction resulting from the poetic genius itself, which sustains and modifies the images, thoughts, and emotions of the poet's own mind." [16] I myself can find a perspective in which I may be said to argue that much of contemporary theoretical criticism is best comprehended as a particular development in understanding this statement by Coleridge, and explaining something of what it can and cannot mean. It would be pointless to speculate whether Wimsatt would welcome a similar perspective to accommodate his own views, but I think few students of modern poetics would account for Wimsatt's opinions in this way. For example, referring to Wimsatt's discussion with his co-author Monroe Beardsley of the intentional and affective fallacies as essays in resistance to "reducing the meaning of the poem to that intended by the author" or "to its capacity to affect an audience," Krieger treats these essays as summational statements by the "new apologists"—that is, the New Critics as brought by Krieger to collective theoretic point in contextualism—of theory of "the poem's independent existence as a world cut off from its author on the one hand and its audience on the other." [17] Thus we see as the most evident aspect of contextualism, considered as a critical position, that it stands in opposition to the Romantic "notion that the poet is a translator of a private, pre-existing idea by which the developing poetic context is restricted and the traditional demands of the medium are sacrificed." [18]

Whether or not Coleridge, in the remark quoted above, intended to present the poet as his own translator, that implication was carried through a century of predominantly Romantic critical practice. Briefly, the notion assumes a split between the poet's vision and his command of linguistic means

[16] Donald A. Stauffer (ed.), *The Selected Poetry and Prose of Samuel Taylor Coleridge* (New York: Random House, 1951), 268.
[17] Krieger, *The Tragic Vision*, 232.
[18] Krieger, *The New Apologists for Poetry*, 75.

by which he may express it; privately aware of what he intends to say, the poet says it in his poem as best he can.

I will not lengthily anticipate my later discussion of the matter in recalling here that, since the early criticism of I. A. Richards and T. S. Eliot, this view of the poet's relation to his poem has been widely regarded as seriously deficient. It is instead our generally shared view that composing is for the poet as much a matter of making or discovering as of translating what he has to say. Also, we think that the poet's findings, as they issue in revision of his manuscript, are better understood as changes in the poem's total organic meaning than as clarification or strengthening of some fully intended, pre-established point or pre-existing vision.

The conclusion of Robert Frost's "Stopping By Woods on a Snowy Evening" is perhaps not only a characteristic but a particularly telling example of discovery in the poetic process, if only because on the surface it would seem that theory of the poet as translator of a pre-existing idea could find no more likely illustration than Frost's composition. The poem was so ready to leap from his mind to the page that Frost wrote it rapidly and with few revisions.[19] But Frost reports of at least the revision by which he arrived at the line whose repetition concludes the poem ("And miles to go before I sleep") that the line took him rather by surprise. That is, on beginning to write his poem, far from being sure where it would come out, Frost suggests that he fell across his conclusion as something of a happy accident.[20]

In so far as that is the case, Frost was learning what he really had to say, for his conclusion is of great consequence to the poem's finished effect. John Holmes explains the operation, line on line, of the final repetition achieved in Frost's revision:

[19] John Holmes, "On Frost's 'Stopping by Woods on a Snowy Evening,'" in R. W. Stallman and R. E. Watters (eds.), *The Creative Reader* (New York: Ronald Press, 1954), 840.

[20] See "A Note By The Editors," in Stallman and Watters (eds.), *The Creative Reader*, 842.

"That's what it was supposed to be—the feeling of silence and dark, almost overpowering the man, but the necessity of going on. 'And miles to go before I sleep.' Then the triumph in the whole thing, the only right and perfect last line, solving the problem of the carried over rime, keeping the half-tranced state, and the dark and the solitude, and man's great effort to be responsible man . . . the repetition of that line." [21]

Here Holmes notes the consequences of Frost's revision for the poem's total effect. We might still more clearly observe the consequences for theory of poetry of that revision, were we to change Frost's conclusion from

> But I have promises to keep,
> And miles to go before I sleep,
> And miles to go before I sleep

to

> But I have promises to keep,
> And miles to go before I sleep,
> For promises I mean to keep!

Even the violate version indicates the necessity of going on. But to notice that merely emphasizes how impossibly stolid it would be to treat the revised poem as only a qualitatively different articulation of the same idea or vision as Frost's original. The substitution effects too great an abomination for that. The "new" poem may or may not say something, but if it does, it is not the same thing said differently but something different which is said.

That so small a change in a poem's anatomy may wreak so large a devastation is of lasting implication for theory of poetry. Surely it suggests how much more reliable and satisfying it ordinarily is to think of a poem's meaning (whatever in a given poem it proves to be) as emerging from the poem's intrinsic details (whatever in words, syntax, and rhythms

---

21 Holmes, "On Frost's 'Stopping by Woods on a Snowy Evening,'" 841.

they may be) than to think of the details as signs of a meaning whose most certain condition is somewhere else, in the privacy of the poet's mind.

Thus we see that the poet's findings are closely related to the poem's meanings; in the process of composition the poet finds what he fully has to say, which is his poem. Holmes describes the actual process in the case of Frost's poem broadly as follows: After some period of mulling over the "actual experience of stopping at night by some dark woods in winter," Frost finally began putting words for a poem on paper. By that time he had already arrived at a notion of what he would say, and he began to say it. But even then—though in that indeterminate phase of mulling, presumably without his having put words on paper, he had begun composing his poem—he had not altogether settled on what to say. That is, even after he had made some changes in his original draft, "the poet knew and did not know how the poem would end," and finally, coming to know how, he finished his poem.[22]

In describing Frost's act of composition, Holmes of course is reviewing the process in the case of only one poem by one poet. Were we to turn to other poems by other poets or perhaps by Frost himself, we would surely discover many differences in detail. A poem might begin in an incident much less directly projected in the piece itself than was Frost's stopping by some woods. It might begin, so far as the poet can introspectively report, in some such slender abstraction from a possible full poetic utterance as a metaphor or even a wordless "tune in the head." But we may reasonably assume that, regardless of their starting points, poets characteristically do not altogether know at the beginning of composition what they will actually say. Even if we did not have poets' introspective reports to this effect, in so far as we observe in drafts of poems changes in the substance of total meaning rather than simple clarification or vivification, we must conclude that poets in

22 See *Ibid.*, 840–42.

significant measure learn or discover or find out what to say while composing.[23]

I do not mean to assert (though I think I believe it of all good poems) that all poems in process represent their authors' finding out what they will say; and I certainly do not insist that poets find in equal measure, for the ability to find a great deal to say in developing his poem may be the mark of a given poet's particular distinction. Here I mean only to note that many poems in process represent their authors' finding out what they are saying and that our assessment of much contemporary literary opinion turns on adequate explanation of this process.

Several of Holmes's observations on Frost's composition of his poem suggest the difficulties involved in such explanation. Holmes says of the feeling effected by Frost's revision near the conclusion of the poem that it then became "what it was supposed to be," a phrase which might be most simply understood as a reference to Frost's prior intention. On the other hand, Holmes's discussion of Frost's process of revision as, basically, the "overcoming" of "one unexpected obstacle"[24] after another may suggest either that Frost's poem in process was a medium resistant to the translation of his ideas or some sort of stimulus or cause of his eventual triumph. Were we to understand Holmes to mean the latter, we might then think him to be saying that the *poem* rather than Frost himself knew "what it was supposed to be." Again,

---

[23] As Krieger reliably reports in *The New Apologists for Poetry* (p. 69), "we find that, in actual practice, poets follow an infinity of methods in working through to the completed poems." But the crucial point for theory depends not on tracing the particular route from inception of a poem to its completion, but on recognizing the finished poem as an "organically unified entity." Then, however the poem began (whether with paper and ink at hand or no), since it could not have begun with the words in their order which is the completed poem, we may reasonably conclude that "the poetic process must be seen as one that does not permit of a pre-existing prose equivalent which is then merely translated into poetry."

[24] Holmes, "On Frost's 'Stopping by Woods on a Snowy Evening,'" 841.

interpreting Holmes along this line, when he refers to the "only right and perfect last line," at a theoretic level this is an assertion that the poem's completion *required* that and only that line; so that, for example, a scientific observer of the poem's language system in process could have predicted the eventual conclusion.

In commenting thus, while expressing confusions of my own, I charge none to Holmes. He speaks, as it seems to me, as we all speak as critics—or at least when we speak like Holmes, interestingly and informatively. My interest is not in criticizing a theory which Holmes does not intend but in remarking the compatibility of some of his comments with contextualism when viewed from the following vantage point. We may well ask: If on beginning his poem the poet does not altogether know what he is going to say, how does he find out? Contextualism may be sympathetically understood as a particular answer to this question; broadly, the poet finds out what he has to say from the work itself, which has its own purpose or intention. According to Krieger, the "new apologists" see the poetic "world", in the perspective of contextualist theory, "as determined by the language context as it evolves partly, of course, under the author's guidance but partly also—and perhaps even more crucially—in response to the demands which the system itself, in developing its own *telos,* creates." [25]

This statement, though it will account for the poet's finding or making, clearly reveals the least happy implication of contextualism. No critic will suppose that several lines of verse on a page can revise or evolve themselves according to their own purpose; obviously the lines themselves do not know if they are about to evolve still further or if they are already in a paradisiacal state of completion. But Krieger's statement suggests such a remarkable incubation.

In noting the apparent assertion of impossibilities, we ob-

[25] Krieger, *The Tragic Vision,* 232.

serve the doctrinal source for the considerable dissatisfaction with contextualism. Criticism ranges from that of anti-New Critics who find New Critics in their contextualist emphasis outrageously "intent on obliterating poetry's relation to life, society, morality, by shutting itself off by itself," [26] to that of a theorist like Krieger, whose is a qualified disapproval. Applauding a contextualist insistence that we "realize the fullness and the complexity of the internal relations of the unique contextual system," Krieger nevertheless fears the effect of a theory which would "keep us inside, bouncing from opposition to opposition" without reference to existence or illumination of "the ordinary world outside." [27] Indeed, Krieger suggests that almost without exception the New Critics, though their analyses lend themselves to systematization as contextualism, personally dissociate themselves from any implication of their speculations which would "isolate" poetry in contextualist privacy.[28] But, however much contextualism is criticized, in the perspective in which we may consider its vulnerability, the wonder is not that it has been sometimes deplored but that it has exerted any influence whatever. In so far as contextualism attributes literal developing *telos* to a poem in process, it merely substitutes for the clumsy view of the poet as his own translator the intolerable view of the poem as its own author—in its linguistic self's absorption uninterested in the world outside.

But if attributing developing *telos* to the poem itself is a literal absurdity which we need not even reject as a point of doctrine, in which no one in fact believes, it does not follow that the notion is irrelevant to adequate theory of poetry. On the contrary, if we understand the notion as a metaphor for the poet's own developing *telos,* purpose, or intention in completing his poem, we may see in contextualism a signifi-

26 Krieger, "After the New Criticism," 186.
27 Krieger, *The Tragic Vision,* 233.
28 See *Ibid.,* 232, 234–35.

cant insight into poetic utterance. The insight is best explained, I think, by a dramatic theory of poetry; in any event it is fundamental to the doctrine of the dramatic speaker.

To reassert, as in dramatic theory, that the poem is the poet's purposeful utterance permits a continuity with the Romantic theory, so satisfying to common sense, that a poet speaks because there is something he wishes to say. But to assert also the developmental nature of the poet's purpose—so in accord with the substantive provisionality evident in manuscript drafts of poems as well as with characteristic introspective reports of poets—permits us to understand his poem as not only the verbal consequence of his purpose; we may also understand the poem in process toward completion as an investigative resource for the poet's fully identifying his intention. That is, the poem's "language context as it evolves" comprises a changing complex of meanings containing various but not limitless potentialities for further ordering.

Probably we cannot offer a more accurate general description of the poem in process considered as an investigative resource for its author. But as it stands the description affords a revealing perspective. If meanings in the poem in process comprise a variety of potentialities for further combination and development, we may conclude that the piece in process does not set a fixed or absolute limit on its author's developing *telos* or intention. Yeats's later massive revision of one of his earlier poems is a spectacular example of the poet's power to reorder his work unpredictably.[29] The early poem seemed completed to its immediate audience; doubtless it seemed so to Yeats himself, who committed it to print. But, finished though

[29] I refer to "The Sorrow of Love," originally published in 1893, but greatly changed in its 1912 publication. In referring to the later version as a reordering I intend a literal, evaluatively neutral description. It is irrelevant to my point in this context that I personally think the later order substantially superior to the earlier. Another critic may judge the later version inferior; this, basically, is Herbert Read's conclusion. See Herbert Read, "The Later Yeats," in Stallman and Watters (eds.), *The Creative Reader*, 842–44.

it was, Yeats could finish it again—the same, yet not the same poem. But proof of the poet's unpredictable invention does not require spectacular illustration, for it is self-evident. We can no more certainly predict what will happen to the poet's poem in process than we can believe, if we deeply approve the finished work, that it could have been written in any other way.

Our sense of a poem's perfection or rightness suggests that, in so far as contextualism implies a literal inevitability in culmination of the poem in process, we best understand the implication as metaphoric description of an effect as a cause. Thus, when Holmes praises Frost's concluding line as "the only right and perfect last line," we rightly understand him to be praising it as Frost's triumph, in the development of his own *telos,* in bringing the poem to an ordered wealth of meaning; but we cannot think that Holmes means, literally, that if we had available all other lines in the poetic system we could predict the certain appearance in it of the only right line. Many evaluative comments exhibit this tendency toward metaphoric treatment of a consequence of the poet's choice as something caused by the poetic system. Our praise of a word in a poem as inevitable, the poet's pleased report of a poem that "wrote itself," though no poem in fact has done so, are examples of the tendency. There is nothing wrong in our speaking so; rather, it is a natural way of praising the achieved work. It is only wrong to extrapolate from our praise of inevitable poetic effects a view of the "language context as it evolves"—that is, the poem in process—as its own creative genius.

But if the poet's own creativity is not absolutely fated by his developing poem, the "language context as it evolves" nevertheless limits the poet's developing intention. At one level I refer to the merely self-evident: A poet may always stop writing or discard a piece he has begun, but to the extent that he *alters* or *changes* it, no matter how greatly, what it becomes will bear noticeable relations with what it has been. If we probe more deeply, we probably find in the notion of poetic limits a rather vague metaphor for a variety of ways in which a poem in a given stage of development or evolution is resistant to change: rhyme or metrical schemes which may, as aspects of the total poem, set fixed limits on what the poet may do in completing them; analogies susceptible to so much and no more linkage. But such matters obviously involve the poet's delicate sense of what he *can* as well as of what he *cannot* do in revision. Thus, the poet attends limitations placed by his "language context as it evolves" as limitations in opportunity.

Reuben Brower refers to the poet's regard for the conditional opportunity for reordering represented by his developing poem as "the writer's vision in action." In context, Brower does not mean the possible Romantic interpretation of the phrase, according to which the poem would be revised to accommodate the poet's full, private vision. Brower means that the poem develops according to what "we can call" the poet's "planning," so long as "we do not suppose it is a simple activity or wholly under 'conscious direction.'" This "important kind of planning" or "vision in action" is Brower's way of referring to the notion of the poet's developing *telos*: "the hidden pressure exerted by the writer's organism to select and relate experience through words, and the further pressure exerted by what is already written, which keeps accumulating as the writer commits himself to particular words and meanings." [30] As Brower's comment, broadly summational of the nature of the poet's *telos,* relates to the poet at work on his poem, I suppose him to be asking as he reviews a given draft of his poem: "If I say what I do *here,* can I (must I, should I, dare I) say what I do *there?*" In developing the poem whose completion is the answer to such

[30] Reuben Arthur Brower, *The Fields of Light* (New York: Oxford University Press, A Galaxy Book, 1962) , 202.

questions, I-the-person who began to compose this piece—under a "pressure" to "select and relate experience through words" which we may accept as "simply 'given' " [31]—becomes "I," the poem's dramatic speaker.

Later we must consider more carefully the poet's affectionate but discerning attachment to his poem's speaker. For the present it is sufficient to observe that attention to the poem's speaker suggests the ground for assertion of dramatic theory as an inclusive alternative to contextualism. In both ways of theoretic regard, "the poem can mean only in the words that constitute it." [32] A contextualist emphasis on the poem's intentionless making leads, probably inevitably, to its being understood as "a self-complicating context with no outside check on the multiplication of complexity heading away from art toward the chaos of romantic obscurantism." [33] But if we consistently attend the poem's words as those of its dramatic speaker, the relevance of questions characteristically put to discourse is necessarily restored. We must ask such questions as: What is the content of the speaker's utterance? Why does he utter it? What does he mean?

In stating in subsequent papers my present opinion on these questions, I am equally or more interested in a large development in oral interpretation and poetic theory of which my personal views are a small part and to which they relate. I see in modern theory a developing effort to deliver a coherent account of the poem as a matter of both saying and making. But, to suggest the full stretch of the development which interests me, I should say that modern poetics works toward a satisfying explanation of the poem as, in the phrase of Wimsatt and Brooks, "a tensional union of making with seeing and saying." [34]

[31] *Ibid.*
[32] Krieger, *The Tragic Vision*, 234.
[33] *Ibid.*, 235–36.
[34] W. K. Wimsatt, Jr., and Cleanth Brooks, *Literary Criticism: A Short History* (New York: Alfred A. Knopf, 1959), 755.

To treat "seeing" as a major component of poetic content has important implications for our understanding what a poem "says." For now, merely to suggest these implications, let us contrast the description by Wimsatt and Brooks with what a nineteenth-century Romantic critic might have offered as a brief formula of the poem: a saying of feeling. The Romantic, of course, understood the poem as its author's highly personal utterance, and I shall urge that there is much in dramatic theory to reinforce a view of the poem as a personal utterance. I see in dramatic theory points of connection with the Romantic movement, whose source in writings in English we customarily attribute to Coleridge and Wordsworth. Indeed, the connections between Romantic and modern theory, in terms both of problems confronted and of solutions forwarded, are strong enough that I think of dramatic theory as a particular development in an evolutionary movement in theory of poetry since Wordsworth and Coleridge.

In nothing else is the influence of Romantic on modern thought more evident than in the contemporary effort to explain the place of emotion in poetry. But, in so far as modern poetics works toward analysis of poetic content as seeing rather than feeling, modern analysis, however evolutionary the process of its arrival, promises a version of poetic meaning which could be but poorly accommodated in the main lines of Romantic thought. Seeing implies observation, insight, recognition, discovery. If analysis of poetic content as a speaker's feeling leads to understanding the poem as expression of pure subjectivity and similar Romantic appraisals, analysis of poetic content as a speaker's seeing leads to understanding the poem as expression of a particular awareness. Thus dramatic theory, understood as an explanation of the way in which a poem is "a tensional union of making with seeing and saying," affords a view something like this: A poem is a report, through the agency of the poet's personally projected (or "made") dramatic speaker, of what the poet has discovered in his engagement with seen aspects of reality. But if the poem is an expression of a particular, subjective awareness, as discovery among things seen it is also objective, a representation of reality.

Surely it is easier for one to say something like this, or even to believe it, than to be altogether sure what one means! Hence, I cannot suppose that my further exposition will answer, or even address, all questions critically affecting a systematic resolution of our regard for the poem as both expression and artifact. But I can hope to contribute to a fusion much to be desired, on grounds of both internal theoretic symmetry and practical effects in analysis of individual poems.

It is not surprising that the oral interpreter will be intensely conscious of the desirability of such a fusion or resolution. He asks for neither more nor less than a coherent explanation for what he knows he himself must do in understanding a poem for his eventual performance of it. Freshly exploring a text which is new to him, he must attend it, as an ordered object, as closely as any other critic; for the exact attention required of him by the poetic text, in the fullness of its detail, is the fact he necessarily confronts if he would communicate the poem with rich precision to others. As oral interpreter, he cannot read themes or ideas but only such Total Meaning as collects in the poem, word by word, phrase by phrase, and line by line. Hence, every nuance of meaning he observes implies a nuance in tone and action in his expressive performance.

Oral Interpretation Doctrine
and Modern Poetics:
The Evolutionary Revolution

$\mathcal{T}$HE title of this paper has been, a friend might say, forced on me, for the revolution of modern poetics against Romanticism has been frequently declared. Those of us whose special interest is oral interpretation of poetry have been much affected—and most of us would say benefited—by the course of this revolution through the past forty or so years. Broadly, we think that we have a better grasp on our aims in analysis and performance as a consequence of the modern attack by the New Critics on the Romantic view of the poem as an expression of emotion.

Whether or not regard for the poem as an expression of emotion is a necessary logical consequence of the Romantic view of the poet as translator of his private vision or intention, Romantic criticism generally has so treated it.[1] Doubtless the suggestion was given a powerful initial impulse in Wordsworth's description of poetry as the emotional residue of the poet's prior personal experience. As Wordsworth describes the relation, "I have said that poetry is the spontaneous overflow of powerful feelings: it takes its origin from emotion recollected in tranquillity: the emotion is contemplated

[1] It would be merely naïve to cite some given volume as containing within itself the fully articulated emphasis of well over a century's critical writings, but it is appropriate to note for its perceptive bearing on theory of poetry M. H. Abrams' omnibus account of Romantic doctrines, *The Mirror and the Lamp: Romantic Theory and the Critical Tradition* (New York: W. W. Norton and Co., 1958) .

till, by a species of reaction, the tranquillity gradually disappears, and an emotion, kindred to that which was before the subject of contemplation, is gradually produced, and does itself actually exist in the mind. In this mood successful composition generally begins, and in a mood similar to this it is carried on." [2] Probably there is nowhere else a more neatly packaged statement than this of the Romantic orthodoxy against which the New Critics revolted. Probably also, as has been pointed out, limiting our attention to statements like the above in Wordsworth fails to credit fully his concern for thought and mind.[3] But this is largely a private question for Wordsworthians, for certainly Wordsworth's position may be taken reliably as "the starting point" for the ensuing "emotional predominance" in poetics.[4] Doubtless the emphasis was reinforced by a general willingness, gathering strength through the eighteenth and nineteenth centuries (and hardly yet concluded) to leave to science the hard, publicly discriminable vision of fact and put poetry in charge of a cloudier sort of vision or idea whose values could be attributed to the power to stir or soothe.

We may suggest the happy effects for interpreters of the modern revolt against treatment of poetry as the poet's overflowing emotion by briefly tracing our changing attitudes to two doctrines, widely accepted even twenty years ago in oral interpretation, which were particularly troublesome. The first of these doctrines, affirming the separability of the logical from the emotional content of a poem, directly affected our analysis of poems. I am unable to trace the steps by which assumption of this separability became a piece of orthodox Romantic analysis, but in our textbooks and general pedagogic practice of even twenty years ago in oral interpretation it was unquestioned. A corollary of this doctrine was that a critical

[2] William Wordsworth, "Observations Prefixed to 'Lyrical Ballads' (1800)," in James Harry Smith and Edd Winfield Parks (eds.), *The Great Critics* (New York: W. W. Norton and Co., 1932), 514.
[3] Smith and Parks (eds.), *The Great Critics*, 498.
[4] *Ibid.*, 497.

précis or paraphrase could preserve intact the thought or rational content of a poem. Such a view obviously implied that a poem is its précis somehow suffused with emotion.[5]

The coarser forms of this view have little remaining influence; they have been washed away in the modern identification of the paraphrastic heresy and the countering argument that the Total Meaning of the poem's particulars cannot be signified in words other than the poem's. This phase of the New Criticism was hardly conducted for the express purpose of aiding oral interpreters, but it might well have been. Permit me to explain by way of a personal aside. Various ones of the so-called New Critics led and chiefly carried the attack on bifurcation of a poem into rational or logical and emotional details. That is the accepted and true view. But as one who was twenty years ago a graduate student and for the first time a teacher of oral interpretation classes, I can report that it was our students and what they were doing, and what we were thinking to suggest that they do in preparing a poem's performance, more than any doctrine of the New Criticism, which deeply dissatisfied some of us with a view of the separability of thought and emotion in a poem. In brief, although we might tell a student to look for the poem's thought or logic *and* its emotion, it was quite clear in observing his performance—as, on introspection, it was quite clear in observing our own—that we were not talking about two contents but one. The thought and emotion were, after all, a closely interwoven attitude or complex of attitudes.

---

[5] I refer to a mode of thought, rooted in Romantic theory of poetry, so widespread among students of literature and interpretation that it was long accepted as axiomatic. Simply to identify its effect on instruction, we may note its appearance in perhaps its most usable context among oral interpretation textbooks, Wayland Parrish's *Reading Aloud* (New York: Ronald Press, 1932), so continuingly useful that the third edition of the book was published as recently as 1953. Parrish advises: "In preparing a selection for reading, one of the best aids in getting at the essential thought is to reduce it to a precis. . . . The finished precis shoud say all that the original says but should say it much more briefly" (p. 43).

My aside's relevance is to speech and oral interpretation students and perhaps, as a footnote, to their historians. It would be erroneous to think that, quite happy with a thought-emotion dichotomy in poetic analysis, we nevertheless got in step with certain developments of the New Criticism in order to illustrate our own modernity, or that we simply made a mechanical application of the latest gadgetry in literary critical terminology.

We were not—some of us were not—at all happy with a view of the poem as its logical précis suffused with emotion. In terms of this view, as instructors we found it hard to put productive questions to the text, or ones proving cleanly applicable to students preparing to perform a poem. As performers ourselves, or as listeners to and judges of performance, each performance-event seemed its own overwhelming refutation of the heresy of paraphrase. I think it idle to speculate whether or not oral interpreters without coaching from literary critics would have developed a vocabulary for analysis sprinkled with such terms and phrases as "attitudes," "language as gesture," and "symbolic action." But it is not idle to note that, when such terms began peeping out of the forests of literary scholarship, we interpreters were ready to pounce on them as consistent with our own experience and as meeting our needs for a more efficient approach to analysis of the poem.

Roughly the same relation holds between literary speculation of the 1940's (and still earlier "new" criticism) and the second point of interpretation doctrine, then widely accepted, which I've said was particularly troublesome. This aspect of doctrine could be and often was summed up in the brief exhortation to the performer, "Respond to the imagery." This piece of advice carried an implication that was, and surely always will be, useful. It points to poetry's characteristic representation of sense-experience—visual, auditory, tactile, kinesthetic, and the like. Indeed, a reader hardly needs to be advised to respond to a poem's imagery; if he reads the poem he can scarcely do otherwise. But "Respond to the imagery," in the context of oral interpretation instruction, was not merely a redundancy; it was something more than a report of just any reader's inevitable experience. The interpreter understood the phrase to mean that his was to be, as interpreter, in some measure a *particular* response, a precise, rich, and full response. So, indeed, the interpreter's response should be—and, rightly understood, "respond to the imagery" will continue to spur the oral interpreter to that particular vibrant relation with his poem which is a requisite of excellent performance.[6] Still, for all its enduring usefulness, the phrase was troublesome, for, in a critical context emphasizing the poem as an expression of emotion, its unqualified directive might seem to open the flood-gates to any and every subjective reaction.[7] If, for example, you think of moles as disgusting little animals leading disgusting little lives, there is nothing in the unqualified "Respond to the imagery" to prevent your intoning with strongly regurgitant expression Elinor Wylie's lines from "The Eagle and the Mole": "Live like the

6 Perhaps the most substantial and provocative discussion of the importance of imagery to the oral interpreter, outside of its relation to the attitudes of the poem's dramatic speaker, is its treatment as an "appeal to the senses" in C. C. Cunningham, *Literature as a Fine Art* (New York: Ronald Press, 1941), 49, and many other passages in the book.

7 The question for us, as oral interpreters, was of course what we should "do" in performance with emotions to which the imagery appealed. In *Reading Aloud,* referring to the poem's "imaginative objects or situations," Parrish notes "that these stimuli sometimes arouse in the reader a similar emotion, sometimes merely sympathy for the emotion expressed, and sometimes a quite different emotion" (p. 371). Hence, as Parrish observes, possibly "we feel pleasure in Burns's loves, we are sorry for Wordsworth's unrest, and in pity we sympathize with Keat's depression" (p. 370). Although these comments may reflect the normal relation of one person's response to another person's emotion, I need hardly emphasize the theoretic difficulties, as they leave us not knowing whether to express, as oral interpreters, our "sorrow" (or whatever response may be ours) or Wordsworth's "unrest," our "sympathy" or Keats's "depression."

velvet mole;/Go burrow under ground./And there hold intercourse/With roots of trees and stones,/With rivers at their source,/And disembodied bones."

Indeed, some interpreters and even instructors of interpretation simply understood the prescription as the reader's permission to take possession of the poem, to use it as desired. But even for those students and instructors who preferred to think of the poem's taking possession of them—and despite the dreadful rumors we have heard about the elocutionists, I think they have always been the majority—the phrase was awkward and cumbersome. One struggled to apply it usefully. First one said, "Respond to the imagery," and the good-natured student did that. Then if he responded, in reading Elinor Wylie's poem, by evoking the presence of a nasty mole, an instructor might say, "Well, very good expression, your mole is very nasty indeed, *but*," and so forth. We hear in this briefly adumbrated scene echoes of classroom discussions we have today and will have as long as there are classes in oral interpretation. But we are more precise than we were twenty years ago in knowing what to say when we get to "and so forth." We ask that the interpreter, as interpreter, respond as the speaker implied by the poem responds; that is, we ask him to respond so as to convey the experience of the person who reveals the motion of his mind and the intonation of his voice through the words in their order in the poem.

The view that the interpreter's responsibility, as interpreter, is to express the poem's speaker's attitudes is, I believe, now a critical commonplace. It does not reduce the value of the principle, although it does complicate the interpreter's task, to observe that the voice of the poem's speaker may express that which converges with, is sharply distinguished from, or, perhaps most frequently, modifies the characteristic ideas and attitudes of its author. If the concept of the poem's speaker is at present a commonplace it is so in some measure because, struggling twenty years ago with the question, "*Whose* response to the imagery shall we express?" we came to discover, in Reuben Brower's happy phrase, the "dramatic design" of poetry.

It will complete my little summary of some leading developments in oral interpretation theory since, say, 1945 to add that in understanding the poem as dramatic discourse we find the basis of the oral interpreter's claim, pressed with fresh vigor in these years, that his subject can play an important role in literary education. In taking this view one defines "dramatic" in a certain sense to mean, as Brower puts it, that "someone is speaking to someone else. For a poem is a dramatic fiction no less than a play, and its speaker, like a character in a play, is no less a creation of the words on the printed page." [8] Briefly, then, if a poem is a dramatic fiction, we can learn much of what the poem *is* if we dramatize or perform it. That is of course the claim, not the argument for it, which is, as students of interpretation know, to be found elsewhere, more or less fully elaborated, in a number of books and articles published in our field in recent years. Here it is sufficient to note the existence of the claim and that it is treated with favor by an increasing number of professors and students of speech and literature.

The character of my remarks on some recent developments may suggest that I am asserting that in the past twenty years we in interpretation have stepped smartly with the New Critics from the darkness of error into the light of truth. I seek other conclusions. Let me, then, prepare for them.

As for contrasts between the immediate past (let us say 1945–50 or, to establish a still safer point of reference, 1940–45) and the present (let us say 1960 to date), there have been some significant changes. We have, I believe, improved our theory of analysis of the poetic text, and we can better direct the student to an efficient reading of a text and to

[8] Brower, *The Fields of Light*, 19.

what his relation to it as an interpreter probably is. In the immediate past it was usual to direct a student to find the logical and emotional contents of a piece and to put them together somehow by phrasing thoughtfully and responding emotionally to the imagery. Today we direct a student to intone the poem as its speaker would intone it, and we suggest that he can discover what that desired intonation is by learning what the speaker think-dash-feels or, more simply, what his attitudes are as revealed by the words of the poem. In the immediate past the responsible interpretation teacher said, "If you would perform the piece well, you must know it fully." Today the interpretation teacher is likely to say, "That's right," but add, "And if you would know the piece fully, start performing it."

These brief descriptions of pedagogic prescriptions and claims of the immediate past and of the present do full justice to neither period. Instruction, whether in 1945 or 1965, covered many more topics than my truncated summary suggests. Furthermore, I do not point to all of the differences, some of them important, between pedagogy of 1945 and 1965. And I do not point at all to the several similarities, many of them important, between oral interpretation study 1946 and oral interpretation study 1966.

I do not mean to treat this matter of similarities in any depth of particularity, although this rather than the matter of our differences is what increasingly interests me.[9] That is,

9 In a discussion in which I frequently underscore my sense of theory of poetry and its analysis as a "seamless web," I shall not emphasize or treat at length resemblances between oral interpretation instruction of the recent past and the present. But it is suggestive to note that in perhaps the most widely adopted introductory college textbook in oral interpretation—Charlotte Lee, *Oral Interpretation* (Boston: Houghton Mifflin, 1959) —its author explicitly grounds analysis of literary structure in Cunningham's description in *Literature as a Fine Art* of "intrinsic" and "extrinsic" factors. But, beyond observing the lively pedagogic influence of Cunningham's doctrine, it would not be hard to establish a context for understanding his work as precursive to emphasis on the interpreter's objective responsibility to express the attitudes of a poem's

I shall not dwell on such particular points of contact as these: One of my own instructors, C. C. Cunningham, would say that he had become an interpretation rather than an English teacher because he wanted to know poems, not the lives and hard times of their authors—thus finding his own way to express a dissatisfaction with the literary education characteristic of his day which led other young scholars in the 1930's to brilliant denunciations and New Critical proclamations in the *Southern Review*. Nor shall I do more than mention the attention paid to cataloging attitudes with suggestions of their importance by Wayland Parrish.[10] And so on. But I must stop at once—or soon I shall be saying what I shall not be saying of Clarence Simon, Frank Rarig, and several other outstanding students of oral interpretation. I will not even ring the changes indefinitely on my discovering the considerable growth in wisdom attained by my instructors during these years in which I myself have been growing older.

Many of the matters I shall not talk about are apposite to a discussion of similarities in instruction and intent between the immediate past and present. But I believe it will be more revealing, as my paper's title suggests, to approach this matter another way—by way of evolution, since that is now legal.

Of course there is something metaphorical or merely roughly analogous in my use of evolution as a descriptive term. But with it I refer to an unconcluded movement in modern

---

intrinsic speaker. To so understand Cunningham would be to cite current emphasis on the performer's uttering the words comprising the poem as its dramatic speaker could be reasonably expected to utter them, as basic explanation of the way in which the oral interpreter attends to making, as Cunningham suggests that he "should" make, "his reading reflect as accurately and completely as possible the art which is in the composition" (p. 264) .

10 I believe a reasonable case could be made that Parrish was one of the first modern students of either oral interpretation or poetry to observe the significance of attitude as an element of poetic *content*. See his discussion of "Attitude" in *Reading Aloud*, 65–76, especially 68–69.

theory of poetry which is not, in relation to Romanticism, simply combative or polemical but continuative. If we cannot predict the culmination of the movement in modern poetics to which I refer as dramatic theory, nevertheless we can assert that there is in it direction as well as motion.

This assertion or judgment derives from some sustained attention to doctrine of the poem's speaker, which has assumed place in modern discussion of poetry as a characteristic aspect of practical criticism of the lyric poem. The critical commonplace opens out on the possibility, indeed the need, for our understanding modern poetics in more evolutionary or continuative relation with Romanticism than can be accounted for by contextualism.

We may reasonably understand contextualism as a theoretic statement drawing together those revolutionary defiances of Romantic analysis by the New Criticism. Hence, we may understand contextualism as, dialectically, the polar opposite of Romanticism, positing against the view of the poem as a personal expression a view of the poem as an object or a system which is "obedient only to the laws immanently within itself," or a "self-complicating poetic context." [11]

But contextualism includes a hint of other, contradictory claims. If in the contextualist regard the poem is a "self-contained" and "unique" system," it is also a "system of discourse." [12] Outside the framework of contextualism we may wonder what else but discourse a poem could possibly be, but within contextualism the notion of discourse is a theoretic eddy swirling against the main current of the argument. For the most evident thing about discourse is not that it is an object or that it is self-complicating, or self-contained, but that it requires a discourser. Thus contextualism takes implicit cognizance of the poem's dramatic speaker. But, once a speaker is admitted into contextualism, the uncertainty of its larger

[11] Krieger, *The Tragic Vision*, 232–33.
[12] *Ibid.*, 232.

claims is manifest. It would be at least awkward if not simply comical to refer to poetic content as a self-complicating object with a speaker in it, yet some such description would seem inevitable if doctrine of the speaker is somehow to be grafted to contextualism.

Rather than attempting this, it would seem simpler and more natural, if we grant that a poem "contains" only in the sense of implying a speaker, to treat the poem as its speaker's discourse and direct our critical inquiry to the content of his discourse and his purpose in uttering it. I myself think this our best approach to reliable theory of the poem. In following it, I think we will find in dramatic theory a development from Romantic theory, including as theoretic gains (and even, to pursue the evolutionary metaphor, mutations) such New Critical insights as have been systematized in contextualism. But, apart from the question of possible findings, approach to the poem as its speaker's discourse so recommends itself to common sense that we may wonder why it has not seemed equally inviting to all modern theorists.

Chief, I think, among obstacles presumed by some critics is that dramatic theory will not prove to be a development, including contextualist insights, from Romantic views but simply a restatement in other terms of Romanticism's expressive theory. At a certain level in general discussion, whether a poem is treated dramatically as its speaker's utterance or Romantically as its author's utterance might seem to make little difference. Also I have suggested, further reducing this difference, that the speaker of the poem in process is characteristically its author determining fully what he has to say; and in course I shall emphasize that there are contexts in which it is largely irrelevant to distinguish between the completed poem's speaker and its author. Such considerations suggest a strong familial or ancestral resemblance of Romantic to dramatic views. But to note the resemblance makes only more recognizable decisive differences in dramatic theory.

Our confidence that dramatic doctrine is truly a development from Romantic expressive theory and not simply its restatement is bolstered by recalling that the same line of thought from which contextualism crystallized as Romantic theory's dialectical opposite or antithesis produced also the notion of the poem's dramatic speaker. Thus dramatic theory turns on an interpretation of this line of thought as an assertion of the poet's rather than, as in contextualism, the poem's developing *telos*, purpose, or plan. There is little likelihood that a theory deriving from this conception will simply repeat the main line of Romantic theory. In the Romantic view, as Wordsworth suggests, the poet, much moved in his experience of a subject of contemplation (for example, a host of golden daffodils), by a process of tranquilly recovering his original excitement, reproduces in his poem the emotion he had formerly experienced. In contrast, dramatic theory depends on understanding the poet's as a speculative probe of experience, in which his poem in process is an investigative resource for his developing *telos* or plan. It should not surprise us, if the notion of the poem's developing *telos* is best understood as a metaphor, that a contextualist critic may suddenly appear as a dramatic critic to observe the poet's explorative interest. Thus Cleanth Brooks, some of whose observations are among the significant critical fund of contextualism, nevertheless says of one poem by one author, but in a context implying general applicability of his remark, "Herrick's process of making the poem was probably a process of exploration." [13] Brooks is referring to Herrick's "Corinna's going a Maying," and the particular example may comfort those of us who will not forswear poetry's emotional impact for the sake of any theory, however immaculate, which seems to deny it. "Corinna" reminds us that we may endure the rigors of dramatic theory and have our emotions, too, for if the poet is a speculative prober his may well be an impassioned speculation.

From a notion of the poet as explorer we derive a particu-

---

[13] Brooks, *The Well Wrought Urn: Studies in the Structure of Poetry* (New York: Harcourt, Brace and Co., 1947), 69.

lar view of the poem as representation. Broadly, it is a representation of the poet's discovery in exploration of a subject of contemplation or aspect of reality (the "what" that may be contemplated). Thus his process of composition is not so much a matter of determining how best to say what he means but, instead, determining fully what he means.

A view of the poem as its author's discovery in exploration of reality is itself a comprehensive metaphor for much that requires our nicer analysis. As for the poet's exploration, doubtless, as Brower suggests, we cannot precisely "explain how vision functions" in the "action" of the poet's developing plan, but "we can point to the order achieved in the completed work." Then "we may assume—and it is a large assumption—that the integrity of imagination experienced by the reader is a sign of a corresponding integrity of vision in the writer." [14] Indeed, this is a large assumption, for in part it returns our versions of poetry to a Romantic regard for the mind of the poet. But also, as Brower states the large assumption, it follows closely the contextualist case for poetry, for if the reader would know the poet's mind he must discover it in the immanent, intrinsic meanings of the poem. Thus we see that the notion of the poet as explorer deeply touches questions affecting the doctrine of the paraphrastic heresy, or the doctrine that a poem's meaning can be restated in paraphrase, its "vision" reconstructed in alternate language.

The doctrine is of course of great consequence for theory of poetry. If poetic meaning cannot be paraphrased, or if it can be but coarsely paraphrased, we find the ground for asserting poetry's autonomy, in the sense that we may claim for it revelations which, in relation to revelations of other forms of discourse, only "poetry can uniquely afford." If a poem's meaning can be restated in other language, we must assume that "meaning and poem are separate entities." [15] In that case it

14 Brower, *The Fields of Light*, 202.
15 Krieger, *The Tragic Vision*, 232, 233–34.

would be our duty, with Platonic fortitude, to turn "meaning" over to the charge of the philosophers (or at least, in these days, to the philosophers of science) and leave the blandishments of poetry to the nurture of verbal illustrators and "damn liars."

Given this sense of the stakes involved in the doctrine of the paraphrastic heresy, we may see that its theoretic accommodation represents simultaneously the prime achievement and the dead end of contextualism. In presenting the poem as a "closed world of meaning" contextualism affords a tactic of resistance to reducing the poem to some other world of paraphrastic meaning. We may assert in terms of contextualism that the "highly wrought internal relations" effected by poetic context create an "utterly unique" total meaning.[16] But with this argument contextualism generates its own curious impasse. In so far as the theory urges that the meaning of a poem depends on and emerges from context, surely contextualism offers not only its own achievement but a vital contribution to any theory which would satisfactorily defend poetry's autonomous nature. But, if emphasis on the importance of poetic context represents the achievement of contextualism, its treatment of the total meaning effected as "utterly unique" suggests contextualism's dead end or "crucial point" [17] in implication. In the framework of contextualist theory of the poem as a "closed world of meaning" which is "obedient only to the laws immanently within itself," we have no alternative to treating the poem's meaning as "utterly unique." But such a view requires our answering questions of fundamental importance for which contextualism makes no provision: If the meaning that emerges from the poem's context is unique, to what in experience does it refer? If poetic meaning is utterly unique, how do we recognize or know what it is?

I fear that in terms of contextualist theory we may turn end-

16 *Ibid.*, 236, 237.
17 *Ibid.*, 237.

lessly on such questions to no conclusion. Yet their adequate theoretic answer would but explain our finest experience in reading a poem and our experiential sense of the relation of what we read to life or reality. As Krieger explains the requirements of any theory which would advance explanation of poetry beyond an emphasis on a "sealed," inviolate poetic context,[18] they certainly include these matters to which ample experience in reading poetry would give testimony. A more richly accurate theory than contextualism would surely show the reader able "to find his way into the poem by its seeming use of ordinary reference, ordinary propositions, and conventional literary forms, only to find himself suddenly and wonderfully trapped by the transmutations that make these elements most extraordinary. And his explorations through this uniquely paradoxical world—at once so full existentially and so rarefied aesthetically—must be seen to show him what is unique about what before, in his blindness, passed as the ordinary world outside." [19]

In sum, Krieger calls for a theory which will provide a defense of poetry's autonomy (by which I refer to its yielding meaning which cannot be translated into some other form of discourse) without seeming to deny its accessibility to readers or its relation to ordinary experience. I think dramatic theory affords a consistent explanation of these matters, but by way of productive hypothesis rather than as final settlement. I personally am reassured to imagine that final settlements in theory of poetry will begin shortly after the last poet on earth has written his last poem. A surmise of this sort permits us to think of a given theory of poetry as a funding for insight rather than as a cause to defend to the death—which is surely well, for the most certain thing about a theory championed on any given today is that it will be some tomorrow's lost cause. So I do not regard dramatic theory as a final truth or as a

18 *Ibid.*, 235.
19 *Ibid.*, 237.

triumphant answer to contextualism, or even—though a developmental perspective is much in my mind—in a military imagery of Advance and Surround. Rather, I think we may more realistically, and with some certainty, say that in contrast with contextualism an approach to the poem by way of dramatic analysis affords a different focus in which we may usefully review some of contemporary criticism's larger concerns. Thus the metaphor offered by a dramatic perspective of the poet as discovering explorer is broadly suggestive: If the words in their order in a poem report the results of the poet's exploration, we may at least hypothesize that he requires just those words in their order to report exactly what he discovers; but, in so far as he discovers something, presumably he arranges his words with intent to reveal the something discovered.

In itself no more than a pretty conundrum, nevertheless this speculation suggests the desirability of our attentive review of the doctrine of the paraphrastic heresy. We may then notice that the doctrine applies with different effect to two planes of the poem's being. In one application it claims that the meaning of the poem's particulars cannot be signified in words other than the poetic utterance. Probably we are more widely agreed on this general proposition than we are on what we actually mean in our agreement; much depends, as I shall subsequently discuss, on our understanding of relations between conception, or sense, and emotion in the poem. But, if the proposition is by no means self-evident, for the present I confine myself to saying that I think it basically true.

In its other application to the poem, on the plane of its theme or thesis, the doctrine of the paraphrastic heresy contains that which is at one and the same time a true claim and an adumbration of a problem that looms large on our critical agendas. This is the claim that what the poem says is not a maxim whose poetic worth of meaning is independent of the poem's particulars. Although there is wide agreement on this view, not even the contextualist, at work in practical criticism beyond the range of his theory's implications, is actually prepared to assume further that the poem simply does not mean. Generally, instead, we puzzle the nature of the poem's meaning. Agreed that the poem is not merely vivid illustration or documentation of a general idea or moral derived from some source other than the poem, we appreciate Brooks's wondering whether "we still want to view the poem as a communication of a theme." [20] Also most of us—certainly I am one—will agree with him that in our paraphrases we cannot "frame a proposition, a statement, which will adequately represent the total meaning of the poem." Thus, like Brooks, and instructed by him, we shall *"not mistake such propositions for the inner core of the poem"* nor "mistake them for 'what the poem *really* says.' " [21]

But, even while assenting to this claim of the doctrine of the paraphrastic heresy, we particularly admire the critics of our own day—Brooks himself one of the more sensitive and penetrating readers among them—for the closeness of their elucidations of the poetic text, so brightly illuminating for us what the poem really says. In the perspective of dramatic theory, I do not think we are forced to interpret this state of affairs—in which, agreed that a poem's meaning cannot be paraphrased, our critics perhaps more vigorously than in any preceding period have labored to illumine the poem's total meaning—as merely a queer contradiction between critical theory and practice, but as a matter which deserves our further thought. For the moment I shall put a line of thought broadly and speculatingly. While we do not wish to treat the poem's meaning as a thematic inner core, we may nevertheless believe that the poem expresses a unified complex of values determined by the author's experiential engagement. Hence, although we shall not try to say the poem in words

20 Brooks, *The Well Wrought Urn*, 65.
21 *Ibid.*, 188.

other than those of the poem, which are the necessary particulars of a valuative representation of experience, we may well state explicitly in our own words the unifying force which is customarily implicit in the poem's total meaning. In subsequent papers I shall discuss this unifying force as its author's discovery or realization of value or significance in his experience of life, which appears in the poem as a dramatized realization: that is, the realization of the poem's implicit speaker. Also I shall suggest that we can best think of dramatized realization as appraisals, including appraisive possibilities ranging from categorical judgments and propositions to uncategorical or tentative assessments or evaluations.

My assumption that so broad a sketch of poetic meaning brings up more questions than it immediately answers is the reason for my continuing discussion. But even the broadly stated conclusion is sufficient to suggest why, as Brooks indicates, "our reading of the poem" is, as is the poet's writing of it, a "process of exploration." [22] In so far as the composing poet intends his poem as a dramatized realization of value in experience, as readers we shall discover this value as it emerges from the verbal representation of particulars of the experience in their variety of interrelations in the finished poem.

A view of the reader of poetry as an explorer but points to our characteristic expectations in comprehending a kind of discourse: speed reading for *Reader's Digest,* slow reading for Milton. But the least implication opens out on larger ones in explaining our need to comprehend poetry slowly.

Anticipating our modern concern with the reader as explorer, as he anticipated so many of our larger critical concerns, Coleridge described the reader's process in an image of joyful excursion—and this may still be, whether applied to reader or writer, the more appealing metaphor, although traveler and explorer meet in their splendid discoveries. As

[22] *Ibid.,* 69.

Coleridge put it, "The reader should be carried forward, not merely or chiefly by the mechanical impulse of curiosity, or by a restless desire to arrive at the final solution; but by the pleasurable activity of mind excited by the attractions of the journey itself." [23] In the perspective of dramatic theory we see that the journey is nothing less than a journey through experience; the journey is that of the poet himself or, more exactly, his projected dramatic speaker of the poem, realizing values in his experience. Hence we do not "shred" the poem to "get" its speaker's "point"; instead we must see what he sees, experience what he experiences, if we would share his realization of values.

Given this view of the reader's exploration, we may appreciate John Crowe Ransom's saying, in a reference to poetic imagery as "true," that "It is probably true in the commonest sense of true: verifiable, based on observation." [24] Such phrasing suggests direct comparison between the descriptive scope of poetry and science. I doubt that the comparison, in terms of positivist conceptions of verifiability as subject to the sanctions of laboratory testing, much advances our understanding of either scientific or poetic representation or designation. But I enjoy thinking that Ransom intended "verifiable" as a metaphor for the power of the understanding reader to see what the poet sees. In any event, we may think of poetic meaning and its verification in existential terms; that is, the poem is one person's articulate report of values discovered in experience which may be shared by his readers. Thus, while not doubting that the poem reports what its author sees of reality, we shall not take his vision to the laboratory for proof. Rather, we shall consider it an addition to the community stock of insights, to make our private possession if we wish to grasp it and if we can.

23 Stauffer (ed.), *The Selected Poetry and Prose of Samuel Taylor Coleridge*, 268.
24 John Crowe Ransom, *The World's Body* (New York: Charles Scribner's Sons, 1938), 156.

This view of the poem as its author's vision of reality through the agency of his dramatic speaker's utterance is surely a benign one. Indeed, it is so appealing that it may seem boorish to analyze it. Yet obviously it differs significantly from a view of the poem as expression of its author's personal emotion. We may best understand these views, I think, as curiously related points in a slowly developing reorientation since Wordsworth and Coleridge in our understanding of the meaning of words in poetry. That this reorientation has hardly moved in a straight line but through a series of vexing problems, hardly yet solved but their character perhaps increasingly clear, is the matter which we shall consider next.

Poetic Meaning:
Some Beginnings
in the Word

SOME part of our understanding the relations between modern poetics, which has been finding its way since roughly World War I, and the Romantic poetics which dominated the nineteenth century depends on identifying Romantic theory as itself a revolution. We may date the moment of this revolution more exactly than is usually the case in tracing ideas. Publication of Wordsworth's "Observations" in 1800 "raised a wall between the Eighteenth and Nineteenth centuries" and "dated a new era." [1] But in submitting this conclusion our histories of literary criticism remind us that the Romantic program was scarcely Wordsworth's private invention, for the seeds of revolution had been well sown in the course of eighteenth-century thought.[2]

In general, the germination of Romanticism bears directly on questions still much with us concerning the nature of poetic meaning. If Wordsworth announced a revolution well prepared in the preceding century, it was prepared by thinkers who, as Ernst Cassirer remarks, characteristically assumed

[1] Smith and Parks (eds.), *The Great Critics*, 496.

[2] See, for example, Walter Jackson Bate, *Prefaces to Criticism* (New York: Doubleday and Company, 1959), 138–39. Recognizing that Wordsworth's *Lyrical Ballads* (1798) and his "famous preface to the second edition (1800) of that book have frequently been cited as signposts dividing eighteenth- and nineteenth-century English literature," Bate observes that nevertheless "in many respects" Wordsworth "simply used and built upon attitudes common in eighteenth-century English thought."

"the union of philosophy and literary thought" and insisted
"on a deep and intrinsically necessary union of the problems
of the two fields of thought." [3] The fact of this assumption explains much about the subsequent Romantic emphasis on
poetry as a content of feeling or emotion, and on our continuing effort in the present to deliver an adequate account of
emotion in poetry. Theory of poetry for the eighteenth-
century pre-Romantic was but one phase of the century's supplanting "the ideal of a purely deductive logic" with "the
ideal of empirical analysis." [4] Walter Jackson Bate puts well
in capsule form the implications of the empirical ideal for
theory of knowledge: "what are called 'universals' are not
objectively existing forms at all, but are merely 'generaliza-
tions' that we make up when we see two or more things
that happen to seem alike." [5] Thus we see that Wordsworth's
"Observations," considered as "a declaration of literary rights,
a powerful document in the liberating of letters from bond-
age" [6] of rigid neoclassic rules, brought to theory of poetry the
developing empirical argument in philosophy: "what we learn
we acquire, not through some abstract rational insight into
'universal' or objective forms, but only through concrete
experience." [7]

Significantly liberating though this direction of thought
proved to be in latter eighteenth- and nineteenth-century
theory and practice—literary and philosophical, political and
religious—it brought with it the questions of what and how
we may learn reliably from experience. By the middle of the
eighteenth century David Hume, "the greatest of British em-

3 Ernst Cassirer, *The Philosophy of the Enlightenment* (Boston: Bea-
con Press, 1951), 275. Cassirer's special interest in this essay lies in analyzing the way in which thought of the eighteenth century, both in
England and on the continent, opens out on major philosophic problems
of both the Romantic nineteenth century and our own.

4 *Ibid.*, 335.

5 Bate, *Prefaces to Criticism*, 103.

6 Smith and Parks (eds.), *The Great Critics*, 495.

7 Bate, *Prefaces to Criticism*, 103.

piricists," had argued powerfully "that if we believe only what *experience* teaches us . . . we cannot actually see or directly sense any real faculty such as reason at all." The argument, adding to the empiricist denial of "objective forms and principles," a doubt of "the validity of the human reason itself," posed the question, "Can we, indeed, know any reality at all except our own subjective *feelings*—feelings that may very well not correspond in any way to outside reality?" [8]

Although I touch only briefly, as a philosophic amateur, on this grave question for philosophy emerging in the very triumph of the empirical "ideal," it is tempting to review in the perspective of the question's implication Wordsworth's doctrine of poetry as the expression of personal emotion. In such a review, acknowledging a prescriptive component in Wordsworth's as in other critics' descriptions of poetry, we may continue to assume that he meant to encourage personal liberation, originality, spontaneity. But we may also think that Wordsworth would have been horrified to think that he was encouraging a view—much affecting the popular conception through more than a century following his observations—of the poet as a disembodied exclamation point floating in search of a daffodil to which it might attach. Rather, if feeling is the one reality of which man may be certain, to call for it as the dominant content of a poem would be to call for such reality as man may know. Add to a notion of this sort faith that to feel naturally puts one in touch with the Deity, and we would seem to have the Wordsworthian position customarily assumed by critics.

In mentioning one among several possible interpretations of Wordsworth's opinion of the worth of emotion, my intention is not to dignify (or reduce) him to a philosopher, after all, but to take still one more critic's notice of similarities between Romantic and modern questions affecting the nature of poetic meaning. As Bate puts it, "the history of philosophy

[8] *Ibid.*

during the nineteenth century and, to some extent, the twentieth century has been an attempt to overcome the difficulties that arose from the empirical philosophy";[9] and when, as historian of literary criticism, Bate measures the extent of empiricist bearings on poetics, he finds one modern movement, its sources in the eighteenth century, "of which romanticism comprises the first stage." [10]

I enjoy a vision of a long sweep of connection in poetic theory from Romanticism to the present, though I should want it to accommodate a view of meaningful modern revolution, too. But we defend our modern revolution poorly to see in it a flat denial of the proposition deriving from the Romantic movement that poetry is the expression of feeling or emotion. To take that course might seem to imply that poetry does *not* express feeling or emotion, a sorry claim which I think no one really wishes to press. Moreover, if outright denial of Romantic claims suggests that modern analysis offers a fully satisfactory alternative to the view of the poem as emotional expression, I fear it is not, certainly not yet, the case.

It is from a superior vantage point that we may argue rather convincingly that modern analysis, itself in a state of development, is modifying the Romantic view of the role of emotion in poetry. In not treating Romanticism as the enemy, we treat it as the progenitor of modern analysis. Not the least of our advantages in doing so is that we assert Romantic doctrine akin to our own analytic embarrassments.

Our shared difficulty is rooted deeply in the mysterious nature of words. We may think of a word as "a sound or a combination of sounds, or its written or printed representation, used in any language as the sign of a conception." [11] This definition offers at least one reliable perspective in which to

9 *Ibid.*, 103–104.
10 *Ibid.*, 99.
11 See *The American College Dictionary* (New York: Random House, 1959).

view matters. A word is one thing; the conception of which it is a sign is another. We recognize the gap between the two when we listen to persons conversing in a foreign language which we do not understand. Is that busy trade in noisy signs truly a human enterprise?

But if we find almost miraculous the gap between sign and conception in languages which are foreign to us, we must think still more miraculous the gap's instantaneous closure in a language which we do understand. We feel the effect all the more keenly in (what we call) our own tongue because the closure is subject to sudden rupture, as when, for example, we must look up a word in the dictionary, some word which is otherwise merely a noise. But, in our immediate consciousness of words which we understand, we do not utter or respond to signs of conception but to the conceptions themselves. Indeed, the invasion of words by conception is so thorough that, as I. A. Richards notes, "we put its meaning into our working definition of a word." [12] To ask how signs and conceptions attach to one another is, as Richards comments on a related matter, to "have half the abstruser problems of semasiology on our hands." [13] On this topic probably all that we can say indisputably is that in practice we "not only *talk* but actually think as though the words and their meaning are one and the same." [14]

The fact of our talking and thinking so permits our attending with refreshed awareness the frequently remarked "preoccupation with the medium" in modern literary thought.[15] Conventionally we refer to the medium as words or as language, or like C. C. Cunningham we may say broadly that the "medium is language, words." [16] Language, which

[12] I. A. Richards, *Coleridge on Imagination* (Bloomington: Indiana University Press, 1960), 107.
[13] *Ibid.,* 104.
[14] *Ibid.,* 107.
[15] See Charles Feidelson, Jr., *Symbolism and American Literature* (Chicago: University of Chicago Press, Phoenix Books, 1965), 45.
[16] Cunningham, *Literature as a Fine Art,* 42.

Eliseo Vivas reminds us consists of "words and syntax," [17] may seem the larger, inclusive term. But once we think of words, as in fact we do think of them, as conceptions it is clear that we define a word by using language. Hence, language—words and syntax—may inform us, if for any reason we want to know, that a woodcock is an Old World snipe-like game bird, with long bill, short legs, and large eyes placed far back in the head. Thus, if we think of words and their meanings as one and the same, whether we refer to the medium of poetry as words or as language or as both words and language, we refer to a medium which is heavily conceptual in nature.

In so far as words are conceptions, fully to understand their character would require exact knowledge of relations between conceivers and what is conceived, and between what is conceived and what is. These are general and profound questions for philosophy of language in its variety of forms, but, since Coleridge's forceful illustration of their more puzzling features, critics have not doubted their relevance to theory of poetry. Conversely, even modest essays in poetics have some bearing on these questions. Thus, in tracing some developments in analysis of relations between the poet and his poem and the closely connected matter of poetic content, I am involved, however tentatively and willy-nilly, in this sort of discussion. In treating the poem as a tissue of words or conceptions which effect the poet's fusion of subjective expression and objective discovery, I imply an understanding of conception in poetry as a kind of perception of reality. It would seem that the kind cannot be explained by the familiar psychological view of a perception of what is really there in objects and processes into which a subjective, distortional element intrudes.[18] Rather, it would seem that we gain insight, in the perspectives open to poetry, into some portion of what

---

[17] Eliseo Vivas, *Creation and Discovery* (New York: Noonday Press, 1955), 76.

[18] See, for example, Maurice P. Hunt and Lawrence E. Metcalf, *Teaching High School Social Studies* (New York: Harper and Bros., 1955), 24.

is really there only in so far as it enters the individual consciousness of the poet and, after him, his reader. Following Cassirer a little length, we account for the subjective element thus. What we (in his happy conception) notice is really there—the objects or processes—but we notice what we do because of our nature as men, or as men of a certain time and society, or as individual persons.[19]

This direction in thought is, as Vivas reminds us, purely speculative even among those philosophers most capable of guiding it, and with relief I now leave their larger problems. Meanwhile, if we are left "regrettably in the dark"[20] on many relevant matters, still other matters of some importance to theory of poetry become more fully visible through our attention to words as conceptions. The conceptual character of poetry's linguistic medium affords useful light under which to review Romantic treatment of poetic content as primarily a content of feeling. The doctrine fits loosely with that which we cannot doubt about conceptions: a conception is *something* conceived. If we cannot say with certain confidence that conceptions represent "pure objects,"[21] we nevertheless recognize that conceptions *presume* to represent objects: "red," "white," "blue," "flag," "star," "crown," and "the cat is on the mat with other impediments."

As Richards elaborates the point, in discussing a poem we "include a meaning as well as the marks on the paper. . . . A meaning is always what we are talking about, never the signs."[22] The "meanings" to which he refers include self-evidently, and most evidently, conceptions stored in our dictionaries and the further developed conceptions effected in the whole context of the poem, to which we may even refer

[19] Ernst Cassirer, *Language and Myth,* trans. Susanne K. Langer (New York: Harper and Bros., 1946). See especially "Language and Conception," 23–43.
[20] Vivas, *Creation and Discovery,* 82.
[21] Feidelson, *Symbolism and American Literature,* 49.
[22] Richards, *Coleridge on Imagination,* 107.

as a "new word." In so far as such reference is metaphoric, we are reminded by Krieger that metaphor itself may strike us as a miracle of fresh conception when it "achieves substantive union in the transfer of properties between tenor and vehicle." [23] As for poetic meter, as Richards would have it and as modern critics in general have been inclined to agree, as part of the verbal context which is a poem, it is "the very motion of the meaning." [24] Hence, Richards prepares the way for a view of the poem as a tissue of conceptions held together "not as bricks by mortar but as the cells of a living organism grow together." [25]

The organic metaphor is yet another way to announce the preoccupation of contemporary poetics, and in due course we shall consider some of its implications. For the moment it is enough to note merely, and negatively, how poorly a doctrine of poetic content as primarily comprising feelings or emotions must thrive when we keep steadily in mind the *certain* conceptual nature of words. The most evident thing about words is not that they declare, "This is how I feel," but that they burble, "Look at that, and that, and that and that and that." Nouns name objects (or our conceptions of objects), adjectives discern distinctive properties of the objects, verbs tell us what the objects are doing, and adverbs help us to observe still more closely what they are doing. We have so few words to shoulder the poetic load which Romanticism would put upon them that we invent them—and poor poetical robots they are, too, which we name Ouch, Oof, and Eek.

The Romantic solution of the difficulty for theory of poetry as emotional expression which is latent in the plainly objective orientation of words proceeds by positing emotive connotations in words. It is to such connotations that Edward Sapir

23 Krieger, "After the New Criticism," 188.
24 Richards, *Coleridge on Imagination*, 111.
25 *Ibid.*, 120–21.

refers in saying: "Most words, like practically all elements of consciousness, have an associated feeling-tone, a mild, yet nonetheless real and at times insidiously powerful derivative of pleasure or pain." [26] Had we only this sentence to represent Sapir's analysis, we might see it foreshadowing assertion of feeling—given man's sorry thalamic nature—as an inevitable or intrinsic component of conception, varying as conception varies and modified or changed when conception is modified or changed. In fact, however, Sapir does not emphasize the implications of the possessive "have" but rather those of the loosely contractual "associated." Sapir explains his view: "This feeling-tone, however, is not as a rule an inherent value in the word itself, it is rather a sentimental growth on the word's true body, on its conceptual kernel." [27] Given this understanding of a word's components, we are hardly surprised that Sapir concludes as follows: "The feeling-tones of words are of no use, strictly speaking, to science; the philosopher, if he desires to arrive at truth rather than merely to persuade, finds them his most insidious enemies. But man is rarely engaged in pure science, in solid thinking. Generally his mental activities are bathed in a warm current of feeling and he seizes upon the feeling-tones of words as gentle aids to the desired excitation. They are naturally of great value to the literary artist." [28]

Well, that is the kind of analysis of words to make the literary artist blink, even perhaps to march out Ouch, Oof, and Eek to defend him as they can. For Sapir's view washes truth and knowledge theories of poetry and their variants down the drain, and the poet is left to practice not a noble art but a gently exciting neural massage.

Doubtless, treating poetry as expression of emotion frequently leads to derogation of the poet in contrast with the

[26] Edward Sapir, *Language: An Introduction to the Study of Speech* (New York: Harcourt, Brace and Co., A Harvest Book, 1949), 39.
[27] *Ibid.*, 39–40.
[28] *Ibid.*, 40–41.

scientist or solid thinker. I myself think this the most probable among possible consequences. But this is not the point I wish to press. The same theory in another perspective may permit denigration of the scientist: For example, many persons in the eighteenth and early nineteenth centuries, saying with Goethe's Faust, "Feeling is all," preferred the expression of emotion to solid thinking as more representative of man's distinctive nature.[29] Again one may, as Matthew Arnold did, suggest a cooperative exercise in function, leaving discovery of knowledge to the solid thinkers of science and the human accommodation of their discoveries to the fine feelings of the poet.[30] No doubt still other orderings of caste are possible.

But, for the moment, my interest in the doctrine is not in its implications but in its intrinsic perplexity. Sapir puts his finger on it. True, in his talk of conceptual kernels and associated feeling-tones, as if these latter were industrial affiliates on whose solvency the parent company cannot count, Sapir exerts a certain dialectical pressure. But his argument, to the

[29] See Bate, *Prefaces to Criticism,* 101–102.

[30] Generally Arnold's mediation of relations between poetry and science has been thought to be more expressive of the nineteenth-century literary man's Utopian hope than accurately descriptive or predictive. It was characteristic of Arnold, for example, to suggest that "the vast majority" of persons feel "the need of relating what we have learnt and known" from science "to the sense which we have in us for conduct," traditionally within the purview of religion but to come increasingly within the compass of poetry, and "to the sense which we have within us for beauty," which is the special province of poetry—See Lionel Trilling (ed.), *The Portable Matthew Arnold,* (New York: Viking Press, 1949), 417. Doubtless it is pointless to predict when it will be finally determined what orders of thought and knowledge will satisfy what the vast majority need. Meanwhile, Allen Tate offers an evaluation which is probably typical among modern critics of Arnold's idea of division of labor between poet and scientist. See Allen Tate, *The Man of Letters in the Modern World* (New York: Noonday Press, Meridian Books, 1958), 35: "While Arnold's poet was extending the hand of fellowship to the scientist, the scientist did not return the greeting; for never for an instant did he see himself as the inert and useful partner in an enterprise of which he would not be permitted to define the entire scope. He was not, alas, confined to the inertia of fact; his procedure was dynamic all along; and it was animated by the confident spirit of positivism which has since captured the modern world."

extent that it is an argument and consequently disputable, clearly points to that which is indisputable: Words, as conceptions, are designative. They may designate objects, classes of objects, processes, relations among objects, but always *something*. Yet theory of poetry as emotional expression, taken neat, implies—indeed declaims—that poetic content represents or is *about* something only incidentally, if at all, and that its point is to express how someone feels about something. Whether, in observing Romantic doctrine thus putting conceptual elements of utterance to the task of uttering "pure feeling" [31] (one of Cassirer's less happy conceptions, it seems to me), we confront a contradiction, a disjunction, or merely a sheer impossibility, plainly we are observing a breach. Closing the breach requires an explanation which will accommodate both the remarkable power of poetry to express and effect emotion, and the powerful attraction of words to objects.

I mean to tread carefully on ground which may easily give way beneath me. The ground I would keep supports a continuity with earlier analysis of which Sapir's as I have quoted him, published in 1921, is a relatively recent part. Yet, as I treat the Romantic doctrine suffusing Sapir's analysis of language, in some aspects relevant to poetry, I also plainly seem to be building soil to support a different and even contradictory analysis. So indeed I am, in the sense that I conceive of the poem, considered as a dramatized realization of quality, starting with the words where *they* start, looking outward. That is, taking the dramatic view, we will assume, for example, that in "Dover Beach" the most evident aspect of the line, "Come to the window, sweet is the night air!", is that the speaker is saying something like this: "Please move your biologically organized and self-directive protoplasm from the area it now occupies to this area from which you can smell the night air, sweet presumably with the scent of flowers, etc., and which you will be able to smell and hence by impli-

[31] Cassirer, *Language and Myth*, 99.

cation to feel something about because this extremely windowy window is open and not shut." Perhaps you do not see immediately the advantage of this way of putting things over that of saying that the line expresses its speaker's lightly affectionate invitation to his beloved. If so, I am not without sympathy for your difficulty. Here I reassert a point of relation with Mr. Sapir. Just as he surely would, I think that the speaker has affectionately invited his beloved to join him beside the window. The point of difference lies here: Analysis of Sapir's sort would seem to require that, to do their proper poetic work, the various words comprising the sentence "Come to the window, sweet is the night air!" combine with the poetically limited intent of conveying affection. That is, in the strictest Romantic view, whatever else may reside in the words of the cited line, the poetry of them is in their affection. The doctrine I am working toward, which I think modern analysis has been and is working toward, is that the speaker says what he says to a fictively real person about a fictively real object and that he says what he says in order to say that. That the speaker feels something in saying what he says will not surprise us, because nearly everybody feels something when he says something.

Consider again Arnold's line. Of course the speaker is affectionate in addressing his beloved; he enjoys the odors on the night air (implicitly, since he's ready to stand by an open window to smell them, he's probably saying that he enjoys the tactile weight of the night air, too, as a breeze, not a gale), and this combination of affection and sensual pleasure makes up the feeling expressed implicitly in the sense of this line. Hence, we will take it as part of our business as readers to identify and empathize with the emotion implicit in the statement. As oral interpreters, we may even think that expressing this emotion precisely is the most demanding part of our task. So there is no question that emotion or feeling is an important aspect of poetic content, and, were we not reading poetry, we would probably think it equally self-evident that feeling is characteristically implicit in what is said. Yet this view of the matter is connected with a reorientation, only slowly developing, in our understanding of a poem's content and function.

One of the most influential contributions to our reorientation was offered in I. A. Richards' concept of Total Meaning, which he elucidated in *Practical Criticism*, published in 1929. Persons of my age or older will remember that volume as about the only good thing that happened in the year of the Great Crash. In Richards' view, "the all-important fact for the study of literature—or any other mode of communication—is that there are several kinds of meaning," and that, as readers, "the Total Meaning we are engaged with is, almost always, a blend, a combination of several contributory meanings of different types." [32] A hawk-eyed reading is not required to detect in this opinion an evaluation rather different from Sapir's of the verbal energies. The difference presents itself shyly by way of suggestive metaphor rather than by dialectical contradiction. But the difference is real and charged with considerable potential. "Conceptual kernels" and their associated feeling-tones assert for poetry at best the amiable alliance for a purpose of a great with a dependent power, whose dependence is complicated by a certain unreliability and disposition to treachery. In contrast, the notion of Total Meaning, understood as a blend of contributory meanings, opens out on a large vista of possibilities, leading us to observation of the poem's organic wholeness, its reduction of meaning in paraphrase, and like perceptions which we have come to regard as critical commonplaces.

Richards identifies four major functions of Total Meaning—sense, feeling, tone, and intention or controlling purpose—

[32] I. A. Richards, *Practical Criticism* (New York: Harcourt, Brace and Co., 1949), 180.

and our awareness of each of them quickens our sense of the substance of poetic as of other discourse. For example, in his treatment of tone (in poetry, "the poet's attitude to his listeners") as "a distinct character in a poem," Richards attributes to the poem's audience a shaping influence on the poem's content. Although, according to Richards, tone is more difficult to talk about than the other aspects of meaning, "its importance may be overlooked. Yet poetry, which has no other very remarkable qualities, may sometimes take very high rank, simply because the poet's attitude to his listeners—in view of what he has to say—is so perfect." [33]

Doubtless this order of analysis requires tactful application to individual poems. Sometimes it is plainly relevant, as in the case of Gerard Manley Hopkins' sonnet which begins, "Thou art indeed just, Lord." Here, directly addressing God throughout the poem, the speaker questions his status in relation to God, his tone changing as his sense of his actual relationship to the Deity changes. In such a poem, in which a listener is explicitly declared, a reader may discern still another listener or body of listeners whom the poet implicitly addresses and who influence the particulars of his

[33] *Ibid.,* 206. The functional aspect of tone as a definition of a critically isolable part of poetic content should be emphasized. As a heading under which to consider the effect on content of the poet's attitude toward his listeners, "tone" is not an unequivocally happy choice. The word, as title for *some* of the poem's effects, too strongly suggests "intonation" which, in performance, is title for the interpreter's oral expression of effects of sense, feeling, and intention as well as of tone. Briefly, the interpreter seeks to intone the poet's attitude toward his subject as well as his audience.

Beyond urging a readiness to accept terminology when, in concrete situations, it is useful and to forego it when it is not, I know of no simple solution to problems in analysis which may derive from Richards' use of "tone." For the oral interpreter, at least, it may often be less confusing to consider the effect on content of the poet's attitude to his listeners as an effect of rhetoric or persuasion. See, for example, Thomas O. Sloan, "Rhetorical Analysis," *The Oral Study of Literature,* ed. Thomas O. Sloan (New York: Random House, 1966), 137–70, especially 158–62.

utterance.[34] Thus we might find (here I shall not speculate whether rightly or wrongly) Hopkins addressing not only God but a secular nineteenth-century audience with a poem of religious faith. Again, the speaker implicit in many a lyric or "I" poem assumes little more (and the likelihood is that the author of such a poem assumes little more) than a vaguely adumbrated listening presence, ready sympathetically to over-hear the poetic utterance. In such poems of soliloquizing cast— and they are probably the majority among meditative, re-flective poems—it may be as hard as it is pointless to dis-tinguish between a poet's attitude toward his listeners and toward, simply, his subject or what he is talking about.

I but touch on possibilities like these to note that Richards' identification of tone as a function of meaning does not re-quire us to force on every poem's content the same measure and kind of effect deriving from the poet's attitude to his listener. Rather, recognition of the function as a general pos-sibility alerts us to its particular effect when and where it may be evident in a poem.

As Richards discusses intention in *Practical Criticism* (as a discriminable effect in utterance of an ulterior purpose, more or less worthy, characteristically controlling or modifying ut-terance), it is more plainly relevant to forms of discourse other than poetry (as, for example, the discourse of some campaigner for public office who, regardless of what he says, primarily intends his utterance to win him election).[35] But, when Rich-ards briefly discusses "a poem's general intention," he antici-pates the lengthy modern discussion of relations between a poetic utterance and its theme (or thesis) or meaning: "With most good poetry more than one look is needed before we can be sure of the intention, and sometimes everything else in

34 See Sloan, "Rhetorical Analysis," 160–61, for discussion of the dis-tinction between the ostensible, or the speaker's declared immediate, audience and the audience comprising the poem's readers.
35 See Richards, *Practical Criticism*, 182–85.

the poem must become clear to us before this." [36] In so far as this brief statement touches on the poet's intention, we must, of course, as we do later, refer the problem to a richer critical context. But in so far as this comment implies that the reader may find in the poem a central organizational significance, Richards points to the need for an adequate theory of themes for a full appreciation of the larger elements of poetic content.

If, in treating meaning as a combination of functions, Richards was turning from consideration of the poem as divisible portions of concept or thought and emotion, he made his bold turn with some lingering. His ambivalence is most evident in his treatment of two aspects of Total Meaning, which he terms Sense and Feeling. Of Feeling he says this—and I do not see how we could or why we should want to improve on it as a functional definition—"Under 'Feeling' I group for convenience the whole conative-affective aspect of life—emotions, emotional attitudes, the will, desire, pleasure, unpleasure and the rest. 'Feeling' is shorthand for any or all of this." Feeling thus defined, Richards has this to say of Sense and Feeling. First, Sense: "We speak *to say something*, and when we listen we expect something to be said. We use words to direct our hearers' attention upon some state of affairs, to present to them some items for consideration and to excite in them some thoughts about these items." As for Feeling, Richards explains it thus: "But we also have some feelings *about these items,* about the state of affairs we are referring to. We have an attitude towards it, some personal flavour or colouring of feeling; and we use language to *express* these feelings, this nuance of interest." [37]

---

[36] *Ibid.,* 206.
[37] *Ibid.,* 181. To my knowledge Richards has not recanted his analysis of Sense and Feeling in discourse, including particularly poetic discourse. That is not to say that Richards' earliest ideas concerning poetry have not altered, for of course that is not the case. I mention the matter here simply to stress that my interest in writing these papers is not to

Observing that Sense and Feeling are "interlinked and combined very closely," Richards provocatively asserts their "mutual dependence." [38] Yet, against the grain of this assertion, he also implies that Sense is that part of a poem which may be better stated in other form.

Note, for example, his analysis of the word "sprawling"— which Richards cites as an example of the "usual condition" of interrelations between Sense and Feeling in poetry [39]—in a line from a poem by G. H. Luce: "O sprawling domes, O tottering towers." By the time of the speaker's utterance of this line it is evident that the domes and towers described are cloud-domes and cloud-towers, and Richards' analysis of Sense and Feeling in "sprawling" assumes the effect of context on meaning. He says of the word: "Its sense may be indicated as an absence of symmetry, regularity, poise, and coherence, and a stretched and loose disposition of parts. . . . The feeling of 'sprawling' here is a mixture of good humored mockery and affected commiseration." [40]

In his little paraphrase Richards offers conceptions of the word's Sense and of its Feeling. Self-evidently his conception of the word's Feeling is not equivalent to the Feeling itself, for we only know the "good humored mockery and affected commiseration" residing in "sprawling" when, reading the word in the context of the poem, we share these feelings. But Richards claims for his paraphrastic conception of the word's Sense, itself a conception, equivalence, and, indeed, greater clarity in designation. Of his paraphrase of Sense, Richards comments: "I have been careful here to use only neutral (or nearly neutral) words, in order not to import the feeling in

---

trace development in theoretical opinions of any given critic; rather, in so far as my concern is with developmental features, the papers follow general lines of development in modern critical thought, of which the full range of Richards' writings constitutes a consequential part and to which his early comments (of the sort I quote here) served as an impetus of continuing moment.

38 *Ibid.*, 209.
39 *Ibid.*, 212.
40 *Ibid.*, 211.

my paraphrase of the sense." [41] In this remark Richards assumes an object to which the Sense in "sprawling" points which can be known independently from Mr. Luce's special feeling for it. Richards assumes two designations—some implicit sense-aspect of "sprawling" is one, Richards' paraphrase is the other—"directing attention" to the same "state of affairs," and he suggests that the paraphrase gives clearer directions because it does not muddle attention to the object with emotive considerations. Extending the evident line of Richards' analysis to the poem as a whole, we would find Richards suggesting that a paraphrase states more plainly the sense in the words of a poem than the poem itself can put it. To the extent that this is accurately to understand Richards, if from one viewpoint we observe in his analysis an emerging stress on organic relations of sense and feeling, from another viewpoint we observe a careful phrasing of the conventional separation of sense from feeling: We are to read Luce's poem to learn his feeling for a state of affairs whose actual character can be best described in critical paraphrase.

The most telling objection to this view is that it depends on an inappropriate application to Sense in poetry of criteria that are applicable to scientific conception. We are well aware that scientific observation of systems and states of affairs requires elimination of personal, subjective distortion, and it would seem that Richards' statement of sense in "sprawling" aims at a riddance of this sort. Thus, since sense is a kind of truth-claim, Richards' analysis of it is in keeping with his positivist assumption that "truth is ultimately a matter of verification as this is understood in the laboratory." [42] Convinced, by the time of his writing *Practical Criticism*, that poetry is an "emotive utterance," [43] Richards perhaps inevitably stated an element of poetic content, the Sense in "sprawling"—which at

---

41 *Ibid.*
42 I. A. Richards, "Poetry and Beliefs," in Ray B. West, Jr., (ed.), *Essays in Modern Literary Criticism* (New York: Rinehart and Co., 1952), 168.
43 *Ibid.*

least seems to be about something happening in some clouds—in "neutral" terms of the sort a scientist might conceivably use were he, for a scientific purpose, to attend the same cloud-properties or qualities.

But, in proceeding in this way, Richards scrambles answers to two questions which, though they are interrelated, are better addressed separately. One question concerns the cognitive value of Sense in poetry, its worth as knowledge. Inquiring into the matter, we might well compare poetic with scientific discourse, ask whether or not poetic statement meets the conditions of scientific statement and, if not, whether it communicates any Sense whatever. But of more immediate relevance to analysis of the parts of poetic content is the question of what sense a poem presumes or seems to communicate.

The second question is logically prior to the first; we should know the kind of sense a poem purports before evaluating its cognitive worth. It is interesting to observe that Richards' paraphrase of "sprawling," implying that the only kind of Sense a poem could possibly communicate would be an impersonal "scientific" statement, is not his sole suggestion in the matter. In contrast, his explicit general definition does not assume for Sense the restricted context of scientific discourse but more broadly implies the existence of Sense in ordinary utterance. "We speak *to say something*" (It's six o'clock.), "and when we listen we expect something to be said." (Did you say it's six o'clock?) "We use words to direct our hearers' attention upon some state of affairs" (Supper's ready.), "to present to them some items for consideration" (You've soup stains on your coat and coffee stains on your britches) "and to excite in them some thoughts about these items." (I'd better take this suit to the cleaners.) Richards' general definition of Sense encourages us to think of it as not only a scientific statement but as that element of personal report or testimony which informs many kinds of utterance.

Thus, if we treat Sense in poetry as in the nature of a personal report, we note that the Sense of the line in which "sprawling" appears lies in its speaker's declaration of qualities. In his perception the cloud-domes are not, as Richards suggests they are, in a stretched and loose condition to which the speaker attaches the label "sprawling" in order to express his good-humoured mockery of the clouds' absence of symmetry, regularity, poise, and coherence. Instead the clouds are quite simply, in the perception of the speaker, sprawling. That is, the speaker is not noting a highly generalized atmospheric feature which the word "clouds" would sufficiently designate. Nor is he noticing merely the clouds' general lack of symmetry, regularity, poise, and coherence. He is not even observing the atmospheric feature which he might observe if he were somebody else. Instead he observes the particular quality available to his own observation, which he designates with a particular and not some other metaphor. What he designates is not crumbling snowmen, the peeling bark of birch trees, or tattered umbrellas, but sprawling domes; and the sprawling domes he observes are not lolling, dawdling, doodling, drooping, or trolling, but sprawling. Or so the speaker says that is what he sees, and in so reporting he would appear to offer a particular "item for consideration" which, as Richards defines the term Sense, is the particular Sense that it is. To think otherwise—that, for example, presenting a crumbling snowman for our consideration would be the same as presenting a sprawling dome—would be equivalent to thinking that any given item of purchase is the same as any other so long as it is bought from the same department store.

We will now consider more closely the question of the particularity of a poem's Sense, noting the effect of our answer on our understanding of relations between Sense and Feeling. Meanwhile we may observe—from my point of view admiringly—that even if there remains a basic uncertainty in Richards' interpretation of interrelations between sense and feeling in poetry, it is his analysis and other analysis of that sort which opens up the possibility for further consideration of the matter. Before one can puzzle the nature of interrelations between sense and feeling one must be convinced that they *are* interrelated. In richly suggesting this possibility, Richards' terms, as John Perry wrote in 1965, "have fairly well established themselves as useful to literary critics." [44]

---

[44] John Oliver Perry, "Analysis and Interpretation of Poems by Varied Means," in Perry (ed.), *Approaches to the Poem* (San Francisco: Chandler Publishing Co., 1965) , 29.

IV Sense and Feeling in the Poem

A satisfying theory of the constitution of the poem will, I believe, include these articles: a given organization of words—that is, specific words in a specific order—cannot be changed into another organization without changing its sense; and the corollary, a given organization of words cannot be changed into another without changing its feeling. In their several formulations, doctrines of poetry as expression of emotion or feeling affirm the corollary and, as they should, with a certain ardor of conviction; but quite as regularly they play truant from directions of the leading article, either by ignoring it or by outright defiance.

Were we ourselves to give testament to such a doctrine of poetry surely we could not do so more plainly yet fetchingly than Robert Thouless. Charlotte Lee, in her book *Oral Interpretation*, quotes him with a delight in which we may share: "In 'The Eve of St. Agnes' Keats has written:

> Full on this casement shone the wintry moon,
> And threw warm gules on Madeline's fair breast.

Let us now try the experiment of keeping these two lines in a metrical form, but replacing all the emotionally colored words by neutral ones, while making as few other changes as possible. We may write:

> Full on the window shone the wintry moon,
> Making red marks on Jane's uncolored chest.

No one will doubt that all of its poetic value has been knocked out of the passage by these changes. Yet the lines still mean the same in external fact; they still have the same objective meaning. It is only the emotional meaning which has been destroyed.[1]

In Thouless' account of what has happened to emotional meaning perhaps there is this or that to quibble with. For example, a certain amusing residue of feeling remains in his lines so that we may observe, even in terms of theory of poetry as emotional expression, a crippled poetic value stumbling among the Keatsian ruins. Still, in the main, Thouless is quite right: his changes in Keats's organization of words somewhat disrupt its expression of feeling.

But Thouless is, I think, a more powerful belter than he claims, for Sense, too, if it is not knocked out, is nevertheless on its knees begging for mercy. Let us honor Thouless' modesty in victory over Sense as far as we can. Let us say, then, even if it is not altogether true, that it is trivial to note that in replacing casement with window he has substituted a genus for a species, for, while all casements are windows, all windows are not casements. Let us even notice, in sympathy for the observer's probably excited condition, that, with a rich, full vision of all that moon-struck virginity before him, he scarcely knows or cares whether the girl is Jane or Madeline. But tolerance in semantic analysis can carry us only so far. When we have collapsed as inconsequential or irrelevant as many differences in Sense as we can, distinctions remain on which we are forced to insist.

Take, for example, the matter of Jane's chest. As Thouless presents it, there is no reason to suppose it a chest of drawers, although it might be, but no reason not to suppose it her hope chest. Or, put in another and more exact manner, the reason we have for supposing that Thouless is not drawing attention to Jane's hope chest is the reason he has smuggled from Keats's different word.

1 See Lee, *Oral Interpretation* 10–11.

But take the smuggled goods, as Thouless obviously intends, for an anatomical substitute, and I am sorry but I must say: Poor, unequivalent substitute it is! I am not now talking about Feelings but about what Thouless refers to as "objective meaning," that which points to external fact. There is, as of course Thouless knows, a still more rigorous sort of positivist questioning which may be addressed to either Keats's or Thouless' lines which puts in doubt whether *either* passage has any relation whatever to external fact.[2] But Thouless evidently posits a more liberal frame of reference in which the words of a poem *might* point to external fact. It is within this frame that he proposes Jane's uncolored chest as a fair trade in objective meaning for Madeline's fair breast.

Such an offer must, we think, derive from an extremely near-sighted view of the merchandise. Forget entirely how you *feel* about the external facts to which the phrases point and which contain their objective meaning. Consider only those matters to which the phrases point; surely they are external facts which are as different, say, as Edie Adams and Phyllis Diller. That I am more enchanted by my Phyllis than by beautiful Edie is the business of my own feelings. But it would be ungentlemanly of me not to distinguish one bosom from the other.

There are still further points of difference between the chests cited by Keats and Thouless. The particular marks on Madeline's particular chest declare some relations and suggest still others. The marks are warm, hence living, and if warm and living somehow a part of, rather than plastered onto, Madeline's own warm, living being. Also they are a certain kind of mark, gules, lines in an engraving, so that Madeline is

2 I refer of course to comments like that of Rudolph Carnap—as quoted by Susanne K. Langer, *Philosophy in a New Key: A Study in the Symbolism of Reason, Rite, and Art* (Cambridge: Harvard University Press, 1942), 83–84—who speaks of "cries like 'Oh, Oh,' or, on a higher level, lyrical verses." In this comment logical positivism, strictly minding its P's and Q's, delivers the ultimate verdict on the ultimate thrust of doctrines of poetry as expression of feeling.

seen as a warmly living engraving—a work of art come to life, so to speak. Also, since we expect to find gules on heraldic shields, there is suggested Madeline's serving under the sign of the moon, thus becoming—given conventional associations of meaning signified by the moon—the sign and symbol of enchantment and romance. And I would venture that, as the words of Keats's lines work on one another, Madeline's warm and vibrant service throws a gule of June across the wintry moon. However it may be in the outer reaches of reference associated with Madeline's fair breast, I am afraid we must conclude that poor Jane's chest, sopped in red marks though it be, has little of external fact to offer except a miserable rash.

Through somewhat elaborate detail I am saying broadly that different words make different sense—just as different words convey different feelings. In saying so, my initial temptation is to apologize for wasting your time in explaining something so self-evident. Yet we know that, in practice, the matter is not at all self-evident. The dictionary informs us that there are words which are synonyms, that is "one of two or more words of the same language having the same or nearly the same essential meaning." [3] Such analysis of the individual word opens up possibilities for full statements being synonymous and, as we know, various philosophers of language have labored zealously to establish necessary conditions for synonymity of statement.[4] That Thouless has his view of the matter,

[3] *Webster's Collegiate Dictionary*, 5th edition (Springfield, Mass.: G. and C. Merriam Co., 1945) .

[4] For examples of issues involved in defining the nature and conditions of synonymity—particularly in relation to interpreting philosophic statements—see Nelson Goodman, "On Likeness of Meaning" (pp. 67–74) ; Benson Mates, "Synonymity" (pp. 111–36) ; and Arne Naess, "Toward a Theory of Interpretation and Preciseness" (pp. 248–69) in Leonard Linsky (ed.) , *Semantics and the Philosophy of Language* (Urbana: University of Illinois Press, 1952) . Students of poetics will note with some amusement that, while apparently it is quite difficult to restate what a philosopher says, Mr. Mates, at least, expresses some confidence that a poem's interpreter need not endure similar hardships: "To interpret a poem for someone is usually to translate the poem into linguistic expressions which he can understand better than he understands the poem."

admitting different statements in possession of the same Sense, is clear enough. And so it goes. Even Richards, as we saw, although his concept of meaning in the poem as a Total Meaning encourages us to suppose that to tamper with one part of the totality is to tamper with other parts as well, nevertheless delivers as the Sense of the word "sprawling" a stretched and loose disposition of parts for which words such as "flaccid" or "rubbery" would seem to do equally well.

Our problem in formulating the relation between Sense and Feeling is a compound of several items, among which these are, I think, chief: agreement that doctrines of poetry as emotional expression have a grip on some part of the truth about poetry's nature, for surely it includes as a mighty power the expression of emotion; a simultaneous dissatisfaction with these so-called Romantic doctrines as being, in one or another respect, in error or partial and incomplete; and, perhaps not least, our awareness, in analyzing poems, of the potentialities in language for devising synonymous relations between words and between statements.

Modern analysis seeks—through an abundant variety of individual critical attitudes, beliefs, and doctrines—a coherent account of these influences. Our tactical or methodological problem, a problem on which it seems to me that modern analysis as a whole is at work, is in sorting out our thoughts concerning these influences. That may be a different thing from saying that modern critics do not know what they think.

Let us notice, as an example of our difficulty in coherently evaluating the general influences I have mentioned, their work-

---

But, continuing his discussion, Mates builds soil—if without specific intent—for a view of oral interpretation as "translation" into a "complex language" of vocal and bodily expression of the poem's gesturing particulars. "Sometimes the translator may find it desirable to use gestures, signs, tears, and other devices in addition to the meaningful expressions of the conversational language. We shall then regard the language into which the translation is made as a rather complex language, consisting not only of written or spoken expressions but also of these various other occurrences." (p. 114.)

ings in the opinions of one critic, Yvor Winters. Of all modern critics Winters is the last we would charge with not knowing what he thinks—with not having his own definite opinion of the nature of the poem or of not stating it boldly and determinedly. Yet the chief sources of our difficulty in stating coherently the poem's nature are very much evident in Winters' thought—indeed perhaps particularly evident simply because his is so much a thumbs-up, thumbs-down critical orientation.

Winters states his general position thus: "The theory of literature which I defend . . . is absolutist. I believe that the work of literature, in so far as it is valuable, approximates a real apprehension and communication of a particular kind of objective truth." Again, more closely observing the poem's nature, he writes: "The poem is a statement in words about a human experience." [5] Surely these propositions may attract the elucidatory or argumentative interest. But, whether we agree or disagree with them, we must admit that these assertions are of an objective disposition. That is the only aspect of their character which, in terms of my present interest in them, I would stress. Mr. Winters' poem is to be about human experience; it is to apprehend a kind of objective truth. Whether this view is more or less sound, it probably is not the same view in which we may understand the poem as a dramatized realization. In juxtaposing these broad formulations I do not mean to invite consideration of their possible points of contrast, but of two major points of similarity or even identity. These formulations voice a characteristically modern program for poetics—or, more accurately, the modern problem. Both formulations emphasize the values of designation in the poem's economy, stressing that it should be the poem's business to be somehow about something; and both formulations are rooted in some measure of dissatisfaction with Romantic theory.

[5] Yvor Winters, *In Defense of Reason* (New York: The Swallow Press and William Morrow and Co., 1947) , 11.

Winters states explicitly his dissatisfaction with Romantic theory of the poem which "assumes that literature is mainly or even purely an emotional experience." Furthermore, he sees this doctrine as part of a large set of ideas repugnant to him. "The Romantics," he says, "offer a fallacious and dangerous view of the nature both of literature and of man." In this comment Winters in effect commits his allegiance to Irving Babbitt and the critical hosts who took arms under his banner to defy one *weltanschauung* and to proclaim another. It is indeed hard to find a critic who has declared more forthrightly and explicitly than Winters his opposition to Romantic doctrine, including the view of the poem as an expression of feeling or emotion.[6]

Winters' detestation of Romantic doctrine makes his qualification all the more vivid. He notes, as I have said modern analysts characteristically note, though not always so explicitly, that Romantic theory takes serious account "of the power which literature seems to exert over human nature"; and in similar vein Winters repeats that the Romantics "offer a relatively realistic view of the power of literature." [7]

But the doctrine of the poem as expression of feeling exerts a greater pressure on Winters' analysis of the nature of the poem than either his declared objectivist position or his complimentary aside in a generally denigratory evaluation of Romantic theory would suggest. Noting that if we are to talk rationally about poetry we should know "what we mean by a poem," Winters states: "A poem is first of all a statement in words. But it differs from all such statements of a purely philosophical or theoretical nature, in that it has by intention a controlled content of feeling." This is to make an inherently Romantic distinction between philosophical and poetic discourse, and Winters' amplification of the distinction only emphasizes its Romantic character. Although "controlled con-

---

6 *Ibid.*, 8.
7 *Ibid.*, 7.

tent of feeling" distinguishes the poem from a piece of philosophical discourse, Winters adds: "In this respect, it does not
differ from many works written in prose, however. A poem
differs from a work written in prose by virtue of its being
composed in verse. The rhythm of verse permits the expression of more powerful feeling than is possible in prose
when such feeling is needed, and it permits at all times the
expression of finer shades of feeling." [8] It is hard to imagine a
more Romantic conception of essential differentiae than these:
the poem is distinguished by its content of feeling from the
philosophical work; the poem, through the agency of its versi-
fication, is distinguished by its greater power and finer nuances
of feeling from prose works sharing the same emotive intention.

We will hardly wonder that, given this understanding of
distinctions, Winters concludes simply, "A poem, then, is a
statement in words in which special pains are taken with
the expression of feeling." Nor will we wonder at his post-
script: "This description is merely intended to distinguish
the poem from other kinds of writing; it is not offered as a
complete description." [9] Indeed we must think that the view of
the poem as "a statement in words in which special pains
are taken with the expression of feeling" would seem something less than a complete description to a critic whose overriding intent is to urge "that the work of literature, in so far
as it is valuable, approximates a real apprehension and communication of a particular kind of objective truth."

To observe the poem, as Winters permits us to or even insists that we see it, feeling its way toward objective truth suggests alternative frames of reference for evaluating his analysis.
Seen in a dialectical perspective, Winters' doctrine of the
poem is a polyglot combination of Romantic content and
Classical intention. I speak of alternative frames of reference;

8 *Ibid.*, 363.
9 *Ibid.*

I mean better and worse frames. Not only do I not urge an evaluative perspective in which we may watch Winters building a doctrinal trap to catch not poetry but himself, but I resist such a perspective as providing an unsatisfactory glimpse of the more useful production under way in Winters' thought as in modern analysis generally. Doubtless there is a certain embarrassment attached to the evolutionist observation post I recommend in preference to the dialectical, for it emphasizes how much easier it is to look backward than forward. Still, I see no reason why thinking on poetry should exempt the human mind from its habitual limitation. Also, I admit to a personal value deriving from the view of modern theory as an evolutionary development. Not only can I, from that vantage point, explain the necessity of other persons' errors; I can forgive my own. It is an advantage not lightly to be forsaken. I refer of course to forgiving myself only those errors I know I am making. I leave it to a future evolutionist of ideas to explain the good reasons for my making all those errors of which I am blissfully unaware.

To an error, then, which I know I am making in my treatment thus far of Winters' thought. But I mean to confess no more sin than is seemly. My error, so far as I know, is not so much one of omission as of precision. My own comments, as I understand them, could be interpreted fairly to mean that in a significant aspect of his thought Winters is but echoing Romantic doctrine. That is not precisely true. To the extent that it is true, then it is an echo with a clarifying difference.

I do not know how Winters himself would define the difference between his own thought, at the point where I invite comparison, and Romantic doctrine. I myself find a difference—a difference which I would call a sharpened emphasis—in his assuring us that a poem's content of feeling is controlled. This is an emphasis not much declared in Romantic writings of the nineteenth century. William Hazlitt, for

example, could write that poetry is not a branch of author-
ship, "that it is instead 'the stuff of which our life is
made.' The rest is 'mere oblivion,' a dead letter: for all that
is worth remembering in life is the poetry of it. Fear is
poetry, hope is poetry, love is poetry; contempt, jealousy,
remorse, admiration, wonder, pity, despair, or madness, are
all poetry." [10] This is a wondrous equation indeed: poetry is
emotion; emotion is poetry.

Well, one cannot be just to everyone, and it remains less
than fair to note merely that this comment does not truly
express Hazlitt's theory of the poem; for he customarily assumed, as Romantic doctrine generally has assumed, that a
poem requires an author. But Hazlitt's comment suggests
the uncontrolled lengths to which a very good critic could go
in 1818 when the subjective Romantic afflatus was full upon
him.

To treat Hazlitt's cited comment as the ultimate subjective
thrust of Romanticism is to be freshly impressed by the
achievement in development signified by views like Winters'
of the poem as "a statement in words in which special pains
are taken with the expression of feeling." Winters urges the
case for emotional control in analyzing in poetic statements
what he calls "the basic unit, the word." [11] He reminds us
that "each word has a conceptual content, however slight,
each word, exclusive, perhaps, of the particles, communicates vague associations of feeling." [12] Sapir has told us just
how vague and flighty those associations may be. What Sapir
calls the conceptual kernel's associated feeling-tone "varies
remarkably from individual to individual according to the
personal associations of each, varies, indeed, from time to
time in a single individual's consciousness as his experiences

[10] William Hazlitt, "On Poetry in General," in Walter Jackson Bate
(ed.) , *Criticism: The Major Texts* (New York: Harcourt, Brace and
Co., 1952) , 304.
[11] Winters, *In Defense of Reason,* 364.
[12] *Ibid.,* 363.

mold him and his moods change." Thus it is, for example, that "if we have browsed much in our childhood days in books of the Spanish Main, [the word] *hurricane* is likely to have a pleasurably bracing tone; if we have had the misfortune to be caught in one, we are not unlikely to feel the word as cold, cheerless, sinister." [13] Winters remarks this vagrant quality in feeling when he comments, "The word *fire* communicates a concept; it also connotes very vaguely certain feelings, depending on the context in which we happen to place it—depending, for example, on whether we happen to think of a fire on a hearth, in a furnace, or in a forest." [14]

But in the poem, says Winters, "these feelings may be rendered more and more precise as we render the context more and more precise; as we come more and more near to completing and perfecting our poem." [15]

Concept, or Sense, has an important role to play in Feeling's coming out perfectly finished. Winters broadly summarizes it thus: "The concept represented by the word, motivates the feeling which the word communicates." As this relationship works out in the individual word, the basic unit of discourse, "It is the concept of fire which generates the feelings communicated by the word." [16] As it works in the context of the whole poem, that order of words we seek to achieve in coming "more and more near to completing and perfecting our poem," the relationship "between rational statement, and feeling, is thus seen to be that of motive to emotion." [17]

In these remarks by Winters there is obviously fare for the student of semantics. I will leave it to him to determine whether the term "conceptual content" equals "rational statement." Given Winters' readiness—a readiness, I believe, more

13 Sapir, *Language*, 40.
14 Winters, *In Defense of Reason*, 363.
15 *Ibid.*, 364.
16 *Ibid.*
17 Winters, *In Defense of Reason*, 365.

than equal to that of any other modern critic—to declare a given poem or passage good or sometimes not so good, perhaps they are not synonymous terms; for it would seem generally that, while for Winters all rational content is conceptual, the converse does not inevitably hold true. But in the particular context I am considering, the essay "Preliminary Problems," in which Winters interchanges the terms "conceptual" and "rational," it is conceptual that he defines—ostensively by pointing to *fire,* which his discussion permits us to think of conceptually as at least flammable material in a state of inflammation. So I think that fire is rational in being conceptual and that Winters intends rational as an equivalent of conceptual.

I would rather analyze Winters' understanding of the relation of concept to feeling. It is a relationship in which there are curious dependencies. Winters declares it a necessary relationship, thus reaffirming Richards' assertion of interrelations between Sense and Feeling. Concept has a certain dreadful power for destruction: "If there is a necessary relationship between concept and feeling, and concept is unsatisfactory, then feeling must be damaged by way of the relationship." [18] The function of concept is to motivate; or, again, the relation of concept to feeling is that of a generator. These and other metaphors that we may think appropriate to the words "motive," "motivate," and "generate" declare the authority of concept, but it is an authority in servitude. The terms point toward results: the public worth of a motivation lies in what is motivated, of a generator in what is generated. And indeed it does appear that Winters understands concept as an instrument of Feeling's power: Whether or not concept is unsatisfactory will be determined by the measure in which it does or does not damage feeling.

Winters spells out the instrumental function of concept in

[18] *Ibid.,* 364.

his discussion of two words and their relations in two lines from Browning's "A Serenade at the Villa":

> So wore night; the East was gray,
> White the broad-faced hemlock flowers.

The objects of Winters' interest in these lines are the words "wore" and "gray," about which he says this:

The verb *wore* means literally that the night passed, but it carries with it connotations of exhaustion and attrition which belong to the condition of the protagonist; and grayness is a color which we associate with such a condition. If we change the phrase to read "Thus night passed," we shall have the same rational meaning, and a meter quite as respectable, but no trace of the power of the line: the connotations of *wore* will be lost, and the connotations of *gray* will remain in a state of ineffective potentiality. The protagonist in seeing his feeling mirrored in the landscape is not guilty of motivating his feeling falsely, for we know his general motive from the poem as a whole; he is expressing a portion of the feeling motivated by the total situation through a more or less common psychological phenomenon. If the poem were such, however, that we did not know why the night *wore* instead of *passed,* we should have just cause for complaint; in fact, most of the strength would be lost." [19]

Given this clear illustration of doctrine, we may understand that for Winters as for Romantic critics generally poetry remains a significant expression of feeling. But for Winters the poem is not merely hope, love, contempt, jealousy, and the like. It is even more than authored words. The poem is a collection of words particularly honored by their author, for they express their Feeling only by being, in their particular order, the particular words that they are. To observe this characterization is to admire Winters for bringing Romanticism to its ultimate show of respect for the poem, declaring the inseparable interrelation between Sense and Feeling in the poem. Indeed, it is as easy for Winters as it was for Cleanth Brooks, generally denouncing the heresy of any and every paraphrase,

[19] *Ibid.,* 365–66.

to say, "The poem communicates so much and communicates it so richly and with such delicate qualifications that the thing communicated is mauled and distorted if we attempt to convey it by any vehicle less subtle than that of the poem itself." [20] It is no wonder that Brooks regards Winters' position as "the most respectable example of the paraphrastic hersey," [21] for, in indicating that the poem's content cannot be delivered in words other than the words in their order in the poem, Brooks and Winters are of one opinion.

Doubtless the ultimate Romantic respect remains less than perfect. We could still more highly commend the poem's eloquence by asserting that its Sense, too, requires the poem's particular words in their particular order. I think modern criticism, including Winters', works toward this evaluation. True, Winters' example in analysis of two words and their relations in the poem by Browning posits that some portion of the poem's conceptual content or Sense could be articulated in other utterance, in words other than the words of the poem. It is this assumption which requires his understanding at least some of the words in the poem as selections, from among conceptually equivalent alternatives, determined by their bearing on the poem's Feeling.

But Winters also states his understanding of the relations of concept or Sense to Feeling in a manner to imply Sense's role in the poem as primary rather than secondary; or, to put my interpretation more exactly, in a manner to imply that Feeling is implicit in, or inevitably attaches to, Sense rather than Sense's being of instrumental importance in the development of Feeling. In so doing Winters also, I think—if with a broad, ambiguous gesture—directs our attention to the poem's making a Sense not to be achieved by other words in other orders.

In his essay "John Crowe Ransom," Winters writes as follows:

20 Brooks, *The Well Wrought Urn*, 67.
21 *Ibid.*, 183.

Now a poem is composed of words; that is, it is conceptual in its origin, and it cannot escape from its origin. A poem about a tree is composed primarily of abstractions, and secondarily of the feelings aroused by those abstractions: the tree, its leaves, its bark, its greenness, its brownness, its roughness, its smoothness, its strength, its motion, and all its other qualities must be indicated in terms which are primarily conceptual. These terms, however, all suggest certain loose possibilities in the way of perception and feeling; and the poet's business is so to relate them, or others similar to them, that a single and definite idea emerges; in company with a mental image of some aspect of a tree, and in such a way that the feeling is communicated which is appropriate to the total idea—image both as a whole and with respect to each detail as one comes to it in reading.[22]

In making this statement Winters does not, as in "Preliminary Problems," puzzle his way through analysis of its terms or illustrate it by a specimen example from a poem. Nor do I mean to exaggerate its difference from Winters' argument, as I have traced it, in "Preliminary Problems." In this statement, as in the other essay, Winters refers to Feeling's determination of word choice. But here Winters would have words chosen to get a feeling appropriate to sense, and Sense moves closer in this passage to something to which Feeling, if it is not yet for Winters simply embedded in Sense, at least fits, as a dress may be said to be more or less appropriate to the body it clothes. Furthermore, and more significantly, Winters makes Sense a determiner of words in the poem, too; they are to be so selected and related in his poem about a tree "that a single and definite idea emerges in company with a mental image of some aspect of a tree." I do not seek to press from this statement more than it affords in support of the poem's irreducible Sense: Winters talks still of similar words from which one can choose; his urging that a single idea emerges from the poem doubtless contains some alternative possibilities for interpretation. Yet certainly this statement encourages us to think of

22 Winters, *In Defense of Reason,* 503.

words being chosen in a poem for the exactitude of their sense as Sense. Or, to put it more cautiously still, Winters' statement here, if it offers something less than encouragement to this view of selection of words for a poem, makes evident the issue affecting its Sense: Are words in a poem selections from conceptually equivalent alternatives?

Our answer depends on what we mean by conceptual or Sense equivalence. I believe it has a rather complex or, perhaps better, elastic meaning. Conceptual or Sense equivalence depends in part on the intrinsic powers of designation of words—those powers which, as Richards says, present "some items for consideration"—and in part on our purposes in uttering or responding to words.

Let us consider first the designative coverage of individual words and of statements made from them. The many obvious differences and kinds of difference scarcely need mentioning for our purposes, even in passing. No one will think that the word *horse* means literally *watermelon* or that the statement "The horse ate the oats" means literally "This watermelon is delicious." That is foolish, and our interest and problem lie in accounting for resembling words and statements. I have cited a dictionary as authority for synonymity, for the existence of words having the same or essentially the same meaning. But the dictionary preserves more than the muddle of our common fund of thought; it also preserves the subtlety. Diplomatically assuring us that synonyms are words having the same essential meaning, the dictionary shrewdly and painstakingly notes difference in designation between or among synonyms.[23] So, for example, we learn that, while *replace,*

---

[23] Dictionaries vary in their manner of indicating the habit of synonyms to desynonymize. The wisdom of *The Shorter Oxford English Dictionary* (3rd edition; London: Oxford University Press, 1962), makes directly explicit both synonymic identity and difference in meaning by defining a synonym as follows: "Strictly, a word having the same general sense, but possessing each of them meanings which are not shared by the other or others, or having different shades of meaning appropriate to different contexts; e.g., *serpent, snake; ship, vessel; glad, happy; to kill, slay, slaughter.*"

supersede, and *supplant* are synonyms, *replace* actually means "merely to take or fill the place of something"; "*supersede* commonly implies the setting aside of what is replaced"; and "to *supplant* is to supersede, esp. underhandedly." In keeping with the dictionary's fine eye for nuance in designation, we replace a loss, are superseded by our subordinates, and read of Jacob's supplanting Esau.

Even synonyms then, those words having "the same or nearly the same essential meaning," retain a certain uniqueness in power of designation. The uniqueness of the power is frequently merely potential; whether or not it is activated depends on our purpose in utterance.

Our question, then, affecting the Sense of the words in the poem, stated for our closest observation in answering, becomes this: Is it the purpose of that utterance which is a poem to press the word toward uniqueness in designation? In the context which is the poem do the small edges in difference of Sense—Sense as Sense, that component in words and statements which would present some items for our consideration and direct our attention to some state of affairs—which separate one word or statement from a word or statement of similar Sense become particularly sharp?

We have Cleanth Brooks's answer in his comment on Winters' analysis of Browning's lines. Brooks argues, "But the word *wore* does not mean *literally* 'that the night passed,' it means literally 'that the night wore.' " He goes on to say that "it is important to see that what 'So wore night' and 'Thus night passed' have in common as their 'rational meaning' is not the 'rational meaning' of each but the lowest common denominator of both." [24]

In declaring difference between the two phrases, Brooks offers us a mathematical metaphor in which to consider their similarity. Both phrases call attention to night's finite duration, but, as Brooks implies, to notice their shared meaning is to see their dissimilarity in sharper focus. To be told that the

24 Brooks *The Well Wrought Urn,* 184.

night passed is indeed to learn that the night was of finite duration. To be told that it *wore* is to learn what sort of finite duration it was, that it held more of pain than of pleasure for the protagonist experiencing it. Briefly, the phrase "So wore night" tells us something different from the phrase "Thus night passed" by telling us all that the latter phrase tells us plus something more.

I am convinced by analysis of this sort that these phrases are not conceptual or Sense equivalents. But the example suffers from a certain complication possibly obscuring its point. Both phrases are substantive, if not precisely grammatical, ellipses for "Thus night passed for him" and "So wore night for him." That is, their Sense—the state of affairs to which our attention is directed—is something going on inside the protagonist. Hence it may be argued still, if with some embarrassment under the weight of Brooksian-like analysis of differences between the phrases, that their only consequential difference lies in what they variously express of the protagonist's Feeling, the Sense-controlled measure of his misery.

Perhaps still more suggestive of the poem's painstaking care for its Sense is a claim Winters does *not* make in discussing Browning's line, "So wore night; the East was gray." It would seem to be logically parallel to Winters' telling us that the verb *wore* means literally that the night passed to say that the adjective *gray* means literally that the eastern sky was of a certain color. But no one would urge that exegetical translation. Indeed, Winters' point in discussion of the adjective *gray* is to emphasize how important it is, in the poem, that the East is gray and no other color. But imagine with me that the East is peach-colored, as it might well be on some dawn finer than Browning's. And in some poem other than Browning's, which shows nature sharing in the mood of the protagonist, we might see such a dawn declaring that nature couldn't care less how miserable one of its denizens might feel.

Yes, a peachy sky would make a great difference to poetic

meaning—a difference this poem does not purpose or allow. With this example we see that resistance of the poem's Sense to synonymization is deeply involved in the question of the poem's meaning. If the poem's Sense is too specific for adequate paraphrastic translation, the most likely reason for its being so is that the poem's author means to make Sense which only the words in their order in the poem can say. The question of the author's meaning in the utterance comprising his poetic text is an intriguing one, to which we may now address ourselves with closer regard for issues involved in answering it adequately.

V
The Poem's
Speaker
as the Poet

$\mathcal{W}$HEN, in a gathering of people, one person, armed with a literary text and with the sinister air of one about to commit a reading aloud, rises to mount the podium, the question is: What is he doing there? Just as, one way or another, his auditors will make clear to the oral interpreter their answer to this question, so will they have their own understanding of its nature. As I am exploring various topics with you in these papers, I would have the question understood—as you may take it, philosophically or even morally, or, as I like to think of it, simply—professionally: What *should* he be doing there? Or, more narrowly, what is the oral interpreter's proper relation to the literary text?

At least one part of the answer to this question will be perpetually valid. Before reading a piece of literature to an audience, the interpreter should understand it. In recognition of human limitations, maybe we should have that principle read: He should understand it as fully as possible. To require perfect understanding might make for more silence than is good for our profession. But, in emphasizing the necessity for an interpreter's understanding the text he reads aloud, we establish general conditions for the identification of a professional heresy. This would be the heresy of exhibitionism, according to which the interpreter would seek to express himself rather than his understanding of the text. All things con-

sidered, I am somewhat grateful for the heresy of exhibitionism. For one thing, in our tactical relations with English de-
partments, it is helpful for us oral interpreters to have a
heresy we can call our own. But I confess that, in coming
down hard on the heresy of exhibitionism, I am striking a
familiar chord. Even Plato, although he had little good to say
about poetry and less for its oral interpreters, did not accuse
rhapsode Ion of not really trying to read Homer as Homer.
But then Plato was a teacher, too, and in the last ditch teachers—despite their pecking at one another on the way to that
last retreat—will stick together. No teacher can earn a living
teaching somebody to express himself. All the student needs
for that is a good set of lungs, and all his teacher needs is
a good set of ear plugs.

So teachers of oral interpretation encourage their students
to understand poems, and other literary texts, in order to
express their content. In that, we take a line which presumably will be followed by future teachers of interpretation.
Certainly it is the line followed by our immediate, as by our
distant, predecessors. But our immediate predecessors could
think of the poem more comfortably than we can as a duality
of contents—thought or Sense, which could be well stated in a
paraphrase, and emotion or Feeling, which it was considered to be the poem's primary intent to express. So, where
they spoke of the poem's content of Feeling, we find it more
satisfying to consider poetic content as a complex of attitudes.

Our immediate predecessors could also think of poetic content as a direct expression of its author, of the poem as an
expression of some part of the poet's emotional autobiogra-
phy. They assumed the poem to be, and admired it for being,
an expression of its author's Feeling. Modern doctrine of
poetry assumes the poem's having a more objective regard for
its author than did Romantic or Georgian critics. Where they
thought of the poem as its author's expression, modern critics
have been freshly impressed, as the critics we call Classical

were impressed, by the poem's being something made by its author. We do not wish, quite, to call the poem its author's contrivance, which smacks more of artifice than art. Neither can we expect widespread approval of reference to the poem, although some of us would accept the description cheerfully enough, as its author's contraption, a figure lacking in essential dignity. We have settled instead on more implicit cognizance of the poem's manufacture through reference to the poem's persona, speaker, or speakers.

For the Romantic critic the poem was an expression of its author's Feeling; for the modern critic, accepting a dramatic emphasis in analysis, the poem is a structure of its speaker's attitudes. If these neat little formulas point to substantial differences between Romantic and modern dramatic doctrines, we have noted too that we may detect some meaningful linkage between them. Doubtless the matter of largest consequence involved in their continuity is in line with our interest in the poem's ontology—its status in and relation to reality. Although we think modern, we struggle, as did the nineteenth-century Romantics in their affectionate care for the poem's constitution, with the question of proper representation. Like them we ask: What of reality, if anything, does the poem represent? Or, if the poem's representative function is nil or inconsequential, in what does the poem's public worth, if it has any, lie? Questions of this sort have been on our critical agendas since the late eighteenth century, when theorists found sufficient cause for probing the Classical doctrine of the poem as imitation.[1] We mean by that primarily the Aristotelian case for poetry. Aristotle, convinced that suprasensible reality required phenomena in which to make its presence manifest, could assume that poetry shows us some part of this process of concrete universalization at work.[2] Today we

---

[1] See Bate's succinct discussion, *Prefaces to Criticism*, 103–104.

[2] Evaluating Aristotle's opinion that "the poet does not simply imitate or represent particular events or situations which he happens to have noted or invented; he handles them in such a way that he brings out

assume a wider variety of possible causes than suprasensible reality for making the poem a concrete universal, but that view of the poem's ontology, or something importantly like it, remains for us a lively option.[3] As considerable a modern critic as Edmund Wilson specifies its meaning, as well as attesting to its value, in stating: "A drama of Sophocles . . . indicates relations between the various human impulses, which appear so confused and dangerous, and it brings out a certain justice of Fate—that is to say, of the way in which the interaction of these impulses is seen in the long run to work out—upon which we can also depend." [4] This is what Mr. Wilson thinks Sophocles is doing, and we may suppose that it is what Sophocles thought he was doing. Indeed, it may

---

their universal and characteristic elements, thus illuminating the essential nature of some event or situation whether or not what he is telling is historically true," David Daiches, in *Critical Approaches to Literature* (London: Longmans, Green and Co., 1956), states: "Aristotle's remarks about probability are perhaps the most germinal sentences in the history of literary criticism." See especially pp. 37–39 on "Imitation and Probability."

[3] We may, for example, attribute our sense of a poem's universal relevance to biological or social and cultural congruences between the experiences of authors and their readers rather than to the workings of suprasensible reality on human materials. Kenneth Burke, in *The Philosophy of Literary Form* (New York: Vintage Books, 1957), writes suggestively: "Critical and imaginative works are answers to questions posed by the situation in which they arose. . . . This point of view does not, by any means, vow us to personal or historical subjectivism. The situations are real; the strategies for handling them have public content; and in so far as situations overlap from individual to individual, or from one historical period to another, the strategies possess universal relevance" (p. 3). Again Burke writes: "Situations do overlap, if only because men now have the same neural and muscular structure as men who have left their records from past ages. We and they are in much the same biological situation. Furthermore, even the concrete details of social texture have a great measure of overlap. And the nature of the human mind itself, with the function of abstraction rooted in the nature of language, also provides us with 'levels of abstraction' (to employ Korzybski's term) by which situations greatly different in their particularities may be felt to belong in the same class (to have a common substance or essence)" (p. 3).

[4] Edmund Wilson, "The Historical Interpretation of Literature," in Ray B. West, Jr. (ed.), *Essays in Modern Literary Criticism* (New York: Rinehart and Co., 1952), 288.

even be what a drama of Jean-Paul Sartre or Edward Albee is doing, whether they think so or not.

I mention ontological considerations touched on previously and to which we will return. For the moment I mean merely to note again that, if we may understand Romantic and modern poetics in dialectical relation to one another, also in certain respects we may understand modern theory as an evolutionary development from Romanticism. Hence, it will not surprise us to find dialectical, or contrastive, and evolutionary, or continuative, impulses simultaneously expressed in modern doctrine of the poem. A significant example of the fusion of influences is reflected in our critical use, in reference to poetic content, of the term "attitude."

Were we not critics of poetry, we would mean by "attitude," our good dictionary may tell us: 1) "Posture; position assumed or studied to serve a purpose, as a threatening attitude"; or 2) "Position or bearing as indicating action, or feeling, or mood; as keep a firm attitude; the feeling or mood itself; as a kindly attitude." [5] Evidently, then, in conventional usage "attitude" may serve simply as a synonym for the feeling or mood itself; for example, a kindly attitude may be something of a motiveless grace, happily bestowed on some persons perhaps to counterbalance the motiveless malignity of the Iagos among us. I need hardly underscore how easily this sense of the term "attitude," as a simple equivalent of feeling or mood, might be taken over by a Romantic critic bent on showing poetic content as an expression of feeling. But the modern critic does not intend a Romantic agreement, for he wishes to declare some interrelations between Sense and Feeling in the poem which cannot be duplicated or fully recaptured in paraphrase. The term "attitude," with some part of its conventional usage pointing to purpose as well as to feeling, or conative response, permits his reasonably carefree adaptation of the word to this critical pur-

[5] *Webster's Collegiate Dictionary,* 5th edition.

pose. "Attitude," as we use it critically, puts a set of feelings into relation with motivating aspects of an object; so that, for example, a man hates war because it is objectionable and loves his wife because she is not. Or something of the sort.[6] As Cleanth Brooks puts it, "the expression of an attitude, apart from the occasion which generates it and the situation it encompasses, is meaningless." [7]

Hence, the term "attitude," as descriptive of poetic content, makes its way into literary analysis as a combinative concept; or, as Monroe Beardsley, Glenn Leggett, and Robert Daniel put it in an introduction for college students to literary study, the term "may cover a good deal of ground; beliefs (moral, religious, political) " and "also includes the speaker's emotions; horror, calm religious faith, ecstatic religious joy, etc." [8] As this example makes clear, it may become hard for the critic, given an inclusive understanding of "attitude," to separate even for purposes of rude illustration Feeling or emotion from belief, thought, or Sense. Beardsley and his co-authors surely do all that can be done in this separative effort in distinguishing simple horror as an emotion from its horrifying cause in thought or belief. But, when they cite as examples of emotion "calm religious faith" and "ecstatic religious joy," we see belief creeping into emotion, Feeling directed by some Sense.

Obviously, then, our critical use of the term "attitude" is dialectically significant as a denial, or at least an enlargement, of Romantic conceptions of the poem as emotional expression. We have found it satisfying, as oral interpreters, to think of

---

[6] Given his purpose to blend Sense and Feeling into "attitude," the critic may take lexical comfort, if not unqualified support, from *The Shorter Oxford English Dictionary,* which reports that "attitude" refers to "a posture of the body proper to or implying some action or mental state" or to a "settled behavior or manner of acting, as representative of feeling or opinion."

[7] Brooks, *The Well Wrought Urn,* 189.

[8] Monroe Beardsley, Robert Daniel, and Glenn Leggett, *Theme and Form* (Englewood Cliffs, N.J.: Prentice-Hall, 1956) , xxv.

the poem as a structure of attitudes or gestures. In analysis of the poem, we think, one more efficiently searches the actuality of poetic content in discovering attitudes, or unified complexes of Sense and Feeling, than by inquiring into the poem's thought or Sense as a component separate and separable from emotion or Feeling. Furthermore, if poetic content comprises, as Brooks suggests, a structure of attitudes or, as R. P. Blackmur would have it, a tissue of gesture,[9] our sense of values of oral interpretation in literary education is heightened. An approach to the poem which emphasizes, as oral interpretation by its nature must emphasize, sensitivity to attitudes or gestures, and to nuances of attitude and gesture, would seem to open an especially promising avenue to close, thorough comprehension of the poetic text.

But to note the reality and consequential implications of the dialectical thrust of the term "attitude" in analysis of the poem does not render irrelevant its lineal, if rebellious, descent from Romantic doctrine. In saying this I do not urge merely the general scholarly relevance of keeping records straight for our histories of ideas. Nor do I mean even that it will be good for our critical consciences to admit modern "attitude" kindred to Romantic Feeling, as it might be good

---

9 R. P. Blackmur, "Language as Gesture," in Kerker Quinn and Charles Shattuck (eds.), *Accent Anthology* (New York: Harcourt, Brace and Co., 1946), 468–70. These few pages, in which Blackmur amusingly recounts his observation of a woman of "French figure" gaining her seat in a bus, by implication carry much of the case for oral interpretation as a valuable aspect of literary study. Stating that "gesture is not only native to language, it comes before it in a still richer sense, and must be, as it were, carried into it whenever the context is imaginative," Blackmur goes on to say, "Nor can we master language purposely without remastering gesture within it." "Performing" a poem, surely, is one of the ways for "remastering" the piece's gestures (which I understand as metaphor or perhaps better, as synecdoche for experiential process, viz., experience-in-process), one of the ways for learning properly how to read a poem. In obvious reference to Blackmur's analysis, Brooks terms poetic structure "a structure of 'gestures' or attitudes" (*The Well Wrought Urn*, 191).

for an aristocrat to confess a great-grandfather hung for a horse thief. No, the relevance to which I refer is not of descent merely but of influence in descent. In noting synonymic possibilities for "attitude" and "feeling" in conventional usage, the dictionary points the relevance. Though we posit the term "attitude" as superior to "feeling" or "emotion" in power to describe poetic content truly, the superior term carries the distinguishable weight of the others.

The commingling of Romantic influence and opposition to Romantic theory may lead to curious results in modern formulation of the nature of the poem. Agreed on the inseparable interrelation of Sense and Feeling in the poem, thereby declaring our opposition to Romantic doctrine, we may nevertheless conclude that the inseparable interrelation purposes a precise expression of Feeling, in which case we would be expressing the Romantic influence. In the preceding paper we remarked one such modern conclusion; here we may note in passing that there is that in the term "attitude," or in the view of the poem as a structure of attitudes, to encourage such a conclusion.

I do not think it an accurate conclusion—not, in any event, a properly stated conclusion—but that is not the point I mean to emphasize. Instead I note this. In so far as modern theory is a development from Romanticism, the contemporary line of inquiry in poetics having noticeable beginnings in the 1920's is itself in a state of incompletion or, if you will and as I think it, in a state of development. We may thus understand widespread agreement in modern theory that Sense and Feeling are inseparably interrelated in the poem. But on the consequent question—broadly, *why* they are inseparably interrelated; whether their interrelations are resolved to serve Feeling or to serve Sense, or, if to serve both, in what manner and with what priorities—we are either disagreed or simply vague. In addressing questions of this sort, modern theory is not a fixed proclamation but rather a developing exploration of relations between Sense and Feeling in the poem; we have already observed something of this exploration which moves, if I am right, in the direction of ever-increasing emphasis on poetry's designative function, not by denial of the expressive function so persuasively enunciated by the Romantics, but by careful regard for its claims.

When I speak of careful regard, I am of course referring to the substantive impact of modern theory as a whole and not to the tone or intent of a given critic. Indeed, I suppose a case could be made that our characteristic expression of careful regard for the truth about the nature of poetic content lies in roundly denouncing one another's errors. If this is the case, let us merely be grateful that in our own, as in earlier eras, literary critics are gentlemen of temper.

However, it is not the gentlemen's tempers but their regard for truth, and the developmental nature of this regard, that is fit subject for our theoretical interest. A significant part of this regard is expressed in modern critical attention to the relation of the author to the poem of his composition.

Dramatic doctrine, implying our necessary attention to the poem's speaker rather than its author, assumes that the poem— and here I am thinking particularly, although of course not exclusively, of the poem written in the first person singular— is a fictive utterance. An important part of dramatic doctrine derives from its immediately precursive "impersonal theory of poetry" as enunciated by T. S. Eliot. As Richards' conception of Total Meaning was the germinal modern influence on our viewing poetic content as comprised of attitudes, so Eliot's conception of an impersonal poetry was the germinal influence on our understanding the attitudes to be structured so as to imply a speaker who reveals just as much of his nature as the poem's structured content permits.

It is our right recollection to think of Eliot's impersonal theory of poetry as determinedly dialectical and anti-Romantic.[10] But he confined the aggressive attack of his salad days on Romanticism within interesting limits. Eliot was of course an avowed if not altogether convicted proponent of Classicism, and in 1923 he wrote: "Those of us supporting what Mr. Murry calls Classicism believe that men cannot get on without giving allegiance to something outside themselves." [11] We would not be surprised to find the author of a sentence like this, his attention turned to poetics, resuming that part of the Classical brief which posits poetry as imitation of suprasensible reality. But that was not markedly Eliot's way of stating his critical opinions. Certainly, as a man giving his allegiance to the Church and as a poet evoking mystic moments in the rose garden, Eliot leaves us ample record of his belief in meaningful traffic between suprasensible reality and the phenomenal world. But as anti-Romantic theorist, Eliot did not argue from theory of poetry as imitation. He accepted the Romantic assumption that the poem's content is emotion; and Eliot expresses both his own Classical emphasis and the focal point of his attack on Romanticism by asserting that the poet is a maker rather than an expressionist of emotion. According to Eliot, "There are many people who appreciate the expression of sincere emotion in verse, and there is

10 Eliot's early readiness for combat is evident in his statement in 1917 of "Impersonal theory of . . . the relation of the poem to its author . . . the mind of the mature poet differs from that of the immature one not precisely in any valuation of 'personality,' not being necessarily more interesting, or having 'more to say' but rather by being a more finely perfected medium in which special, or very varied feelings are at liberty to enter into new combinations." In this passage in *Selected Essays 1917–1932* (New York: Harcourt, Brace and Co., 1932), 7, Eliot says "How immature!" of those qualities most prized under the Romantic dispensation which had dominated poetics for more than a century. As Abrams reports in *The Mirror and the Lamp,* for the Romantic critic the first test of the poem was " 'Is it sincere? Is it genuine? Does it match the intention, the feeling, and the actual state of mind of the poet while composing?' " (p. 23) So it was that Eliot challenged the literary establishment of *his* day.

11 Eliot, *Selected Essays,* 15.

a smaller number who can appreciate technical excellence. But very few know when there is an expression of *significant* emotion, emotion which has its life in the poem and not in the history of the poet. The emotion of art is impersonal." [12] There is a considerable amount of interpretive literature on the nuances and sometimes confusion and even contradictions in Eliot's literary opinions. In citing the foregoing passage I have omitted consideration of some of these nuances and confusions, which can be noted even in the limited context of the single essay ("Tradition and the Individual Talent") from which I have here quoted. But in quoting Eliot as I have, I have pointed accurately to that which broadly separates Eliot's from, say, Wordsworth's theory of poetic content. Against a view of the poet recording in his poem, by way of surging overflow, a prior life-experience of emotion, Eliot presents the poet making or constructing, from various elements of emotion or feeling, a new emotion in his poem.

The point of contact between impersonal and dramatic theory—let us rather say the influence of impersonal on dramatic theory is quite clear: each considers the poem's content as constructed or formed. The dramatic critic, like the impersonalist who influenced him, will busy himself with "emotion which has its life in the poem and not in the history of the poet," though, as we have noted, the dramatic analysis will take account of attitudes of which emotions or feelings will be a component.

But developmental differences from impersonal theory of the authorial relation also attach to dramatic theory. The differences most evidently derive from dramatic theory's doctrine of the poem's speaker.

My use of the term "developmental" is deliberately ambiguous. There are contexts in which it is appropriate to urge dramatic theory dialectically against impersonal theory, as impersonal theory was delivered against Romanticism. But

12 *Ibid.*, 11.

in other contexts it will be appropriate to think of impersonal theory as one phase and dramatic theory as a closely related but still later phase of an evolutionary movement in theory of poetry since the late eighteenth century. The developmental differences to which I would call attention in dramatic theory point to both dialectical and evolutionary ways for our understanding them.

We may best understand these developmental differences by stating the substantive crux of Romantic, impersonal, and dramatic doctrines of poetic content. In Romantic doctrine, the poem is an author's expression of his emotions or Feeling; in the impersonal theory, the poem is an author's construction of Feeling; in dramatic theory, the poem is an author's construction of a Speaker's expression of attitudes.

Dramatic theory corrects or refines, according to whether we view matters in a dialectical or an evolutionary perspective, impersonal theory's account of the relation of the author to his poem in two significant respects. One affects our criteria for worth of a poem, and the second affects our understanding of relations between the poet's biography and meanings in his poem.

As for criteria of poetic worth, dramatic theory, in contrast with impersonal theory, offers the more liberal imposition of terms. I personally must regard this as both correction and refinement of Eliot's doctrine; it is in any event a distinguishable difference.

Some part of Eliot's statement of the impersonal theory had a purpose which theorists and poets today, of whatever party, must surely commend. Eliot's nearest opponent was not a Wordsworth or a Coleridge in the fine flush of his own Romantic rebellion against a doddering neoclassicism, but the Georgian poet making his characteristically saccharine Romantic summation. This body of poetry, which for the youthful Eliot would have been contemporary verse in English, seemed to be saying with one small voice, "While on my

way to World War I, I had the following most joyous encounter with a bluebird." Some sort of jolt to theory of poetry
was needed, and, writing in 1917, Eliot provided the jolt with
his famous dictum: "Poetry is not a turning loose of emotion, but an escape from emotion; it is not the expression of
personality, but an escape from personality." [13] But, though
I am sympathetic with the immediate dialectic purpose of this
comment, as with others like it in Eliot, I think we find its
tone less classical and austere than merely dry and wrinkled.
Taken out of historical context, this statement is not a theory
of poetry; it is a motto for Organization Man. Some part of
the impersonal theory's practical effect on the evaluation and
practice of modern verse was to encourage an academic poetry
embodying, quite unlike Eliot's own poetry, neither distinguishable personality nor emotion.

Dramatic doctrine of the speaker is not a nostrum prepared
for weak poets who would be stronger; but neither does it
imply, as did the impersonal theory, that a poem is the jail
cell of a faceless prisoner. Rather, the doctrine of the dramatic speaker would welcome into poetry all varieties of
personality willing to put their trust in the discipline of dramatic form to achieve their full and distinct articulation. In
saying this, I contrast dramatic and impersonal theory dialectically: the dramatic case for amplitude is the better one.
I believe this to be true. But also, I do not find it hard to
think that, were he writing today, Eliot would urge some such
reinterpretation, and revision, of the impersonal theory of
poetry; and I find it impossible to imagine present understanding along the lines of dramatic theory without Eliot's
and other of his similarly inclined contemporaries' ideas in
poetics.

The second important point at which dramatic and impersonal theories of poetry invite comparison is in their treatment of relations between the poet's person—his general at-

[13] *Ibid.*, 10.

titudes and their development, and specific experiences in his life—and the meanings in his poems or in any given one of his poems.

The question affecting our understanding of the poem's meaning which is addressed to the authorial relation is this: Do we need to know anything of the poet's biography to understand the meanings in his poem? The question, of course, would presuppose our knowing or learning, prior to their interrelation in the poem, the conventional meanings of its words. For modern poems the dictionary should usually suffice, and for the conventional meanings of certain words in poems of an earlier century we would need to search more deeply.

I know of no argument to date which would permit either dramatic or impersonal theory, held to strictly logical account for their shared emphasis on the poem as an intrinsically revealing world of discourse, to answer anything other than a flat "No" to this question. That is, the strictly logical dramatic or impersonal answer, on the basis of reasons given for the doctrines, would be that we do not need to know anything of the poet's biography in order to understand his poem thoroughly.

I do not think that claim, in these exclusionist terms, a justifiable one. Nor do I think that acceptance of dramatic doctrine of the fictive speaker compels us to urge it. But, if I am right in this, it is not because modern theory has dispatched Romantic doctrine of expression but because it is slowly explaining its point within a fuller and more coherent account of the poet's relation to his poem. We see beginnings of what I take to be an inclusive development in Eliot's own writings, despite his impersonalist views, in his introduction into his criticism of the concept of the "objective correlative" and in his manner of discussing it.[14]

It has been widely assumed that Eliot means that the poem

14 See "Hamlet," *Selected Essays,* 121–26, especially 124–26.

itself is an objective correlative of the poet's own emotion. An interpretation of that sort would have Romantic poets expressing their emotions with abandon and Eliotic-Classical authors expressing *their* emotions carefully. That is, of course, a difference, but one somewhat lacking distinction in combat. Hence—as Eliseo Vivas, believing that this is what Eliot means, and as R. P. Blackmur, believing that this is not what he means, equally demonstrate—such an interpretation of the objective correlative rather thoroughly messes up Eliot's Classicism.[15]

But there is a question more important to theory of poetry, if not to elucidation of Eliot, than whether the objective correlative is metaphor or doctrine, or whether it does or does not disturb the symmetry of his views.[16] The more important

15 See Vivas, *Creation and Discovery*, 175–89, especially 175–76; and R. P. Blackmur, "from 'In the Hope of Straightening Things Out,' " in Perry (ed.), *Approaches to the Poem*, 271–73. As Vivas puts it, "The fact that Eliot holds this doctrine shows that, in spite of his avowed classicism, he accepts with the vast majority of his contemporaries the modern dogma that the artist is primarily concerned with emotion" (p. 176). Rejecting interpretation like Vivas' of Eliot's opinion in the matter, Blackmur writes: "The inconsistency with his other notions about tradition and order and behavior and belief would make the acceptance of the objective correlative as a doctrine for poetry impossible even in a mind with such deeply divided allegiances as Eliot's" (pp. 271–72). Blackmur does not indicate why inconsistency is incompatible with deeply divided allegiances, but his conclusion notes as firmly as Vivas' that the objective correlative as doctrine is a warped weapon for the arsenal of a combative classicism.

16 We can be grateful for *both* Vivas' and Blackmur's interpretations; in juxtaposition, mutually correcting one another, they point clearly to Eliot's ambiguous treatment of the objective correlative. Vivas writes in *Creation and Discovery*: "On the surface the notion of the objective correlative seems clear enough. Devised to explain how the poem expresses the poet's emotion, it also asserts that the poet organizes his sensibility through the act of expression. The poet expresses his emotion by 'finding . . . a set of objects, a situation, a chain of events which shall be the formula of that *particular* emotion' which he wishes to express, 'such that when the external facts . . . are given, the emotion is immediately evoked,' (pp. 175–76). In "from 'In the Hope of Straightening Things Out,' " Blackmur rejects interpretations of this sort of Eliot's explanation of the poet's use of the objective correlative: "Eliot was making a metaphor about Shakespeare's failure, as he saw it, to give

question is whether or not his strictest claim, cited above, concerning significant emotion means that emotion expressed in the poem has no consequential relation to emotion in the life of the poet. I enjoy thinking that—if only as a projec-

---

the right words and actions in the right relation or sequence to express the emotions and feelings that were already there in Prince Hamlet, in his mind and the impulses of his behavior. It was not, as I see it, a metaphor about the poet's own relation to *his* feeling and emotion and to *his* language" (p. 271). Blackmur's comment accommodates very well the immediate example by which Eliot illustrates the objective correlative: "The only way of expressing emotion in the form of art is by finding an 'objective correlative'; in other words, a set of objects, a situation, a chain of events which shall be the formula of that *particular* emotion; . . . If you examine any of Shakespeare's more successful tragedies, you will find this exact equivalence; you will find that the state of mind of Lady Macbeth walking in her sleep has been communicated to you by a skilful accumulation of imagined sensory impressions; the words of Macbeth on hearing of his wife's death strike us as if, given the sequence of events, these words were automatically released by the last event in the series" (*Selected Essays*, 124–25). Thus far Eliot's discussion might be offered as an exemplary specimen of impersonal theory's analysis of the poem as skilled construction of the feeling of its characters. But, immediately following the sentence from Eliot just quoted, his discussion continues with a growing emphasis on the emotions of the *author*, thus providing substantial support for interpretations like Vivas'. Eliot continues: "The artistic 'inevitability' lies in this complete adequacy of the external to the emotion; and this is precisely what is deficient in *Hamlet*. Hamlet (the man) is dominated by an emotion which is inexpressible, because it is in *excess* of the facts as they appear. And the supposed identity of Hamlet with his author is genuine to this point: that Hamlet's bafflement at the absence of objective equivalent to his feelings is a prolongation of the bafflement of his creator in the face of his artistic problem. . . . nothing that Shakespeare can do with the plot can express Hamlet for him. . . . The levity of Hamlet . . . is the buffoonery of an emotion which can find no outlet in action; in the dramatist it is the buffoonery of an emotion which he cannot express in art" (pp. 125–26). Eliot next briefly discusses "the intense feeling . . . exceeding its object . . . It often occurs in adolescence; the ordinary person puts these feelings to sleep, or trims down his feelings to fit the business world; the artist keeps them alive by his ability to intensify the world to his emotions. . . . We must simply admit that here Shakespeare tackled a problem which proved too much for him. Why he attempted it at all is an insoluble puzzle; under compulsion of what experience he attempted to express the inexpressibly horrible, we cannot ever know" (p. 126). I think it obvious from these quotations, as from the entire passage from which they are extracted, that Eliot provides ample grist for the mills of *both* Blackmur and Vivas.

tion of my own scruples, though of course I shall wish to scruple over attitudes rather than emotions—Eliot himself did not wish to claim so much, despite his overriding intention to stress the importance of the poet's craftsmanship and the large powers of the poem to determine the perimeter of its own meanings. So I personally, at least, enjoy understanding Eliot to be qualifying his emphasis on craftsmanship, the making of "a new thing resulting from the concentration of a very great number of experiences," when he notes further that "it is a concentration which does not happen consciously or of deliberation";[17] and I enjoy thinking him to be pointing to some interconnection between the significant emotion in the poem and emotion in the life of the poet when he says of Shakespeare's writing *Hamlet*, "Under compulsion of what experience he attempted to express the inexpressibly horrible, we cannot ever know. We need a great many facts in his biography. . . ."[18] I am much less bothered to think that comments of this sort in Eliot blunt his effectiveness as a trooper against Romanticism than I am pleased to think them qualifications he makes in the direction of a true account of the poetic process and the relation of poet to poem. Or perhaps, equally in the interest of truth, I should say that Eliot sometimes hints at what I take to be questions, rather than embarrassments, which become clearer in the perspective of dramatic theory, its emphasis falling on the poem as a fictive utterance.

In so far as Eliot's discussion of the objective correlative and other remarks of the sort suggest meaningful interconnection between the poet's life-experience and his poem's meanings, I see nothing in dramatic theory as such to accommodate a superior qualification. But that does not quite mean that impersonal theory and dramatic theory flounder in the same ditch. We may better figure their relation in the tuning in of a radio signal. Dramatic theory more clearly

17 Eliot, *Selected Essays*, 10.
18 *Ibid.*, 126.

tunes in the signal, in the sense that it provides a more evident context for statement of the biographical question—and, to the extent that this is true, we may hope to work toward a clearer reply. As my preceding discussion amply suggests, it is also quite reasonable to consider impersonal and dramatic doctrines, in reference to this question, as earlier and later aspects of a continuous process of tuning in the same signal.

What my figure illustrates is this: The implicit issue addressed by impersonal theory was whether the poem is the poet's expression or making of Feeling. The biographical question became rather obscurely involved in discussion of how it was that the poet made Feeling. Dramatic theory, in its assumption that what is made is a speaker's expression of attitudes, permits direct statement of the biographical question or issue: Is poetic content the author's personal utterance—his personal confession, reverie, preachment—or is poetic content a fictive utterance?

As Cleanth Brooks notes, dramatic emphasis on the poem's power to deliver its own meanings through the utterance of its speaker or persona "raises the whole question of the relation of criticism to biography." [19] Raises it, let us say, to where it is a plainly visible, important, and even disturbing presence. Brooks puts the question to a poem by Wordsworth in stating his specific point of interpretive disagreement with Donald Stauffer. Brooks writes: "Is the experience of 'On Westminster Bridge' to be considered *as a poem*—the dramatization of an experience (real or imagined, or with elements of both) in which the poet may make what use he cares to of contrast, surprise—even shock? Mr. Stauffer's objection seems to be the conviction that the man-made city was a part of nature, was arrived at slowly in Wordsworth's own life, and therefore he feels that this conviction cannot come to the protagonist as a flash of intuition—cannot come to the protagonist with some sense of shock." [20]

19 Brooks, *The Well Wrought Urn*, 200–201.
20 *Ibid.*, 201.

Doubtless Brooks, in his eagerness to show the speaker in a state of shock, somewhat overloads the point at issue in his own favor by seeming to suggest that only his own way of looking will permit recognition of Wordsworth's poem *as a poem*. But, making allowances for Brooks's partisan emphasis, we may see in his statement a succinct summation of our broad alternatives in understanding poetic content as either its author's utterance or its protagonist's or speaker's utterance.

It is the either/or that bothers us—even those of us who would urge a central reliability and usefulness in the doctrine of the speaker. In "On Westminster Bridge" the speaker just *is* surprised by his sudden sense of the city's relation to nature, and not to see that reaction, for whatever reason, is to miss a significant portion of what the poem says and means. In simple fairness to Stauffer it should be noted that, although he may suffer some astigmatism, he is not really blind to the speaker's flash of insight.[21] But the point of interest to theory is that many another reader, by knowing too well Wordsworth's biography, might be blind to the flash of insight in his poem. Hence, to my mind Brooks's example demonstrates the usefulness of the doctrine of the speaker as a general proposition. It corrects the temptation, indulged at all levels of literary education and sophistication, to replace readings of meanings plainly in the poem with meanings parallel to those uttered by the poem's author in some other context, or to make replacements on the basis of some other extrinsic cause. We are all familiar with this: from the freshman who begins reply to the question, "What does he mean *here*?" with "Well, since Whitman was a pro-Union Quaker, etc."; to the distinguished

---

[21] As Brooks quotes him in *The Well Wrought Urn*, Stauffer does not deny Wordsworth's flash of insight but its critical treatment by Brooks: "[In Brooks's account] Wordsworth's flash of insight—that even a man-made city participates in the life of nature—becomes not a part of a powerful conviction slowly achieved, as Wordsworth himself describes it in *The Preludes*, but an analyzable paradox" (p. 200).

literary man who insists that *Moby Dick* is *not* full of all those metaphoric and symbolic meanings because it is not a poem but a novel;[22] or to the scholar who asserts that *Moby Dick is* full of symbolic meanings because Melville wrote in an age full of symbolistic writers.[23] But it is pointless and wearying to list the inexhaustible variants of the projective temptation; or perhaps I should refer to it as a massive withdrawal symptom, for it must sometimes seem to us that readers have made a compact to look everywhere and at everything but the poem to discover its meanings. The doctrine of the poem's speaker does not cure temptation to withdraw attention from the poem in order to understand it, but it does give us a good medicine to resist the impulse, whether it be our own or another's.

So, if in some measure the doctrine of the speaker is a pedagogic convenience, it is a convenience which we may well think necessary. But educational utility depends finally on substantive reliability. This principle reminds us that even a necessary convenience, unless it is properly managed, may, like the telephone, scatter rather than concentrate attention. And there is a sense in which the doctrine of the speaker, while a reliable account of an important aspect of poetic content, is a truth requiring proper management.

Our need for right management derives from the fact that frequently the author of the poem is strongly committed to what its speaker is saying. Those of us who appreciate the coverage in accuracy and implication of dramatic doctrine will read with pleasure a dramatist comment like that by Brooks and Wimsatt, "Once we have dissociated the speaker of the

22 W. Somerset Maugham, *Great Novelists and Their Novels* (Philadelphia: J. C. Winston Co., 1948).

23 Newton Arvin, "The Whale," in Philip Rahv (ed.), *Literature in America* (New York: Meridian Books, 1957). Arvin asserts that in Melville's time "the poetic mind in America was already symbolist in everything but program" (p. 169). In citing Maugham and Arvin, I exaggerate the opinion of the former less than that of the latter in parodying recognizable orders of critical response.

lyric from the personality of the poet, even the tiniest lyric reveals itself as drama." [24] But our pleasure in this comment will be all the greater for not thinking of any specific tiny lyric, or at least thinking of the tiniest specific lyric possible. For, as soon as we begin thinking of specific pieces, a certain discomfiture attaches to strict interpretation of the doctrine of the poem's speaker, a discomfiture proportionate to the measure in which specific authors attach themselves to their poems.

I intend no mystery in noting a simply recognizable phenomenon of relations of poets to their poems' speakers. Shortly, I shall discuss the authorial attachment, as part of my intent to explore its best critical accommodation. For the moment, to lay the ground for discussion, I merely illustrate the fact of attachment in a vivid and, I think, self-evident example. Wilfred Owen's World War I poem, "Dulce et Decorum Est," begins with the lines:

> Bent double, like old beggars under sacks,
> Knock-kneed, coughing like hags, we cursed through sludge,
> Till on the haunting flares we turned our backs,
> And toward our distant rest began to trudge.
> Men marched asleep. Many had lost their boots,
> But limped on, blood-shod. All went lame, all blind;
> Drunk with fatigue . . .

The poem continues throughout in the same personal, autobiographical vein. To insist that these lines be understood as the utterance of the poem's speaker rather than as the utterance of Owen himself would be, if I may say so, an offensive show of critical swank. It is poor use indeed of good doctrine to so stuff it into the poem that it mutes our hearing Owen's own horrified and angry voice.

At one level I am merely saying sensibly and prudentially that whether, be it in classroom or other critical discussion, we

---

[24] Wimsatt and Brooks, *Literary Criticism,* 675.

speak of poetic content as the utterance of the speaker or of the author will depend in part on the particular poem and in part on the particular critical problem under consideration. But this marginal note for a prudent pedagogy is based on a substantial theoretical assumption. The doctrine of the speaker as definitely points to the problem of the poet's relation to his tiny lyric as to explanation of that relation. The broad outlines of both the problem and its explanation are, I think, as I indicated in my first paper, fairly clear. The mind of the poet informs his poem; his poem reforms the poet's mind. That is a sufficiently catchy comment to be recognized at once as description by crude analogy of the poet's *telos,* which itself is a kind of metaphor for that which remains to be more fully explained.

That will be the poet's creative syndrome—the process by which, intending to express himself about something, he learns through making up his poem exactly what he intends to express. Also we must think, on inspecting revisions of poems, sometimes the poet even learns in making his poem exactly what it is about that he means to say.[25]

We cannot know how precisely and comprehensively future critical analysis may explain the poet's developing *telos*. It is likely that, in our admiration of the poet's finished work, we do not even altogether *want* to know every mysterious turn of his vision in action. Meanwhile, for lack of still more acute explanations, we have in dramatic theory of the poem as the utterance of its speaker that which is richly suggestive. Dra-

[25] Richard Ellmann, *Yeats: The Man and the Masks* (New York: Macmillan Co., 1948), 142–44, offers an intriguing example of a poem's locating its theme over a period of years and through many revisions. Ellmann traces Yeats's working with painstaking care as he changes his poem from—briefly put, and coarsely—the utterance of a love-lorn speaker to one determining to face time's corrosive flux with heroic courage. Ellman, his particular interest being the technical development of Yeats's revisions of the poem, observes: "Only by infinite patience did the poet achieve such skill in his art" (p. 144). It would be equally accurate to say that only by infinite patience did Yeats discover exactly what he meant to speak about, and what to say.

matic theory is both honorably and helpfully suggestive—leaving it to poets to make poems and suggesting that readers read them as, in the finished texts, they are written. When we intone the utterance as its speaker would intone it, whether *sotto voce* or in full voice, as the poet's readers we will have learned with him what he meant to say.

VI

Dramatic Theory and the Poet's Biography

$\mathcal{D}$RAMATIC doctrine of poetry is self-evidently useful to teachers of oral interpretation. Under the guidance of its good judgment, we get right down to cases with the beginning student. Taking up one of the tiny lyrics that dramatic theory teaches us to think of as little dramas, we put to the beginner's heart of darkness the anatomical questions: "You see those words there? Well, how does the speaker implied by the poem intone them?" We then give brisk marching orders: "Now you intone them the way the Speaker does."

As eager as his student to release individual intelligence and passion into oral performance, an instructor may add: "Say the poem as its dramatic speaker would—if he were you saying what he says." But, in thus referring a poem to the student's personal articulation, the instructor will hope to encourage whole response in embrace, not abandonment, of the poetic text. Hence he may have still another formula affecting controls exercised by the poem's dramatic speaker on individual performance: "If he were you saying what he says, how would *he* feel? *You* express that."

Prescriptions like the foregoing call for the student's cunning empathy. If for a giddy moment the neophyte interpreter thinks, "You mean that's all I have to do?" a moment may follow shortly after in which he thinks miserably, "You mean I have to do all *that*?" That will be the moment at which the instructor, his sympathy welling from his own performer's share in the student's misery, introduces the principle of approximation. The principle posits that within himself the interpreter has effectively reconstructed the fictive or dramatic speaker's attitudes as they ripple from word to word and line to line in the poem. The interpreter then reads the poetic utterance aloud, in trust that his perceptive auditors, making cordial corrections in his delivery, will hear what the interpreter has heard from the poem's speaker. Perhaps, indeed, in imaginative response to efficient performance the listener may hear the intonation of the poem's dramatic speaker with a specially concentrated delight of recognition. If, prior to its oral performance, the listener is familiar with the poem, he may even hear that which he can enjoy as fresh insight; that is, a performance may direct his attention to meanings which he had not previously experienced so exactly or entirely. Certainly the interpreter, as artist or maker of an appropriate intonation, will hope to evoke in his listeners the pleasures of recognition or fresh discovery of the poem's meanings. But, whatever else may be said for the principle of approximation, the oral interpretation instructor needs it when he changes from friendly guide into snarling examiner. Under the rule of approximation, A stands for "About right," C is for "Catch the speaker if you can," and F is for "I should have taken Music Appreciation."

If dramatic theory of poetry is functionally useful for oral interpreters, we also have a stake in its offering an adequate general description of poetic content. If a poem is the utterance of its dramatic speaker's attitudes, in major respects its oral interpretation is an instructive model of what we are doing, or should be doing, when we read poems in silent privacy. The oral interpreter tries to effect what any good reader of poetry must experience: the likely intonation and behavior of the dramatic speaker uttering the poem. The able silent reader must in a meaningful sense perform the poem, internalizing attitudes of the poem's speaker. Thus, practicing toward effective oral interpretation of a poem is an unfolding revelation of the experience of proficient reading, as the achieved performance itself is a unique test of precision and probability in interpretation of the whole poem.

But, although dramatic theory is useful pedagogically to oral interpreters, and although it supports our conviction this side of fanaticism in the value of our subject in study of poetry, we do not praise dramatic theory for the regard in which it holds our labors as oral interpreters but for its regard of poetic content. As we have seen, in one sense dramatic theory is an omnibus term for a slowly cohering and frequently puzzled core of insight into the nature of the poem—particularly the lyric or short poem, the poem uttered in the first person singular, whose content the nineteenth-century Romantic critic attributed to its author's Feeling. To understand dramatic theory as a cumulative account of critical insights prepares us, without diminishing our sense of its present usefulness and descriptive values, for the possibility of further development in the theory. Probably dramatic theory has not attained final articulation in its formulation of the poem as a structure of its fictive speaker's attitudes, nor has it probably, in that formulation, completed the arc of its impulse to reveal the poem in the perspective of designative as well as of expressive intent.

In the preceding paper I touched on two points at which we may usefully consider dramatic doctrine afresh. One point involves the term "attitude." An evident difficulty attaches to its emotive overlay which admits the possibility of the term's simple Romantic reinterpretation as a synonym for feeling. But that is not, I think, a consequential problem. We understand that in general contemporary critical practice the word "attitude" asserts inseparable interrelations between, as Richards defines the terms, Sense and Feeling. But that is the limit of the descriptive claim of "attitude." As we have noted, the claim, of theoretic consequence, is useful to students of oral interpretation as to other students of poetry. But it remains something less than the suggestion that in the poem Feeling is implicit in Sense, an assessment which declares not only the interdependence of Sense and Feeling but something further concerning the nature of their interrelation. In this view of the poem we regard its content as a tissue of perceptions and appraisals in which emotions inevitably inhere. Hence, there may be further value in our reviewing Brooks's report that "the characteristic unity of a poem . . . lies in the unification of attitudes into a hierarchy subordinated to a total and governing attitude." [1] I personally find that a highly satisfying description of a poem's unified content. Yet, at the same level of generalization, we may perhaps still more clearly conceive of poetic content as the unification of perceptions and appraisals—or, if you will, of appraisive perceptions—into a hierarchy subordinate to a governing appraisal, which in due course I shall discuss as a realization of significance. To put it briefly, I imagine theoretic and pedagogic contexts in which rather than referring to the poem as a complex of attitudes we may more certainly term it a complex of appraisals.

Doubtless this view of the poem's making a certain sort of Sense in which Feeling is inevitable because inherent derives from understanding the poem as its author's cognition of quality and value. It is easy to call the poem a personal cognition—quite as easy as to call it its author's expression of feeling. But our knowing what it means to think of the poem in cognitive or representational terms requires our reexamination of a second point of dramatic doctrine: the relation of the author to the fictive speaker and hence to his poem's meaning.

As we have observed, the concept of a poem's speaker as somehow distinguishable from its author has its source in impersonal theory of poetry. Impersonal theory, in its emphasis on the poet as maker, invites sharply contrastive comparison with theory of the poet as expressionist. "Probably, indeed," wrote Eliot, "the larger part of the labour of an author in composing his work is critical labour; the labour of sifting, combining, constructing, expunging, correcting, testing: this frightful toil is as much critical as creative." It might be argued that Eliot conceived of the poet as an Horatio Alger hero, a hard-working maker of successful poems. Certainly Eliot urged his view in direct opposition to "the thesis that the great artist is an unconscious artist." In context, Eliot declared this a "whiggery" thesis, but I assume that he was also thinking of Shelley's account, in his famous figure of the fading coal, of the unconscious process of poetic composition.[2] Shelley wrote: "A man cannot say 'I will write poetry.' The greatest poet even cannot say it; for the mind in creation is as a fading coal, which some invisible influence, like an inconstant wind, awakens to transitory brightness; . . . Could this influence be durable in its original purity and force, it is impossible to predict the greatness of the results; but when composition begins, inspiration is already on the decline, and the most glorious poetry that has ever been communicated to the world is probably a feeble shadow of the original conceptions of the poet." [3]

One almost wishes for the sake of simplicity that these passages from Shelley and Eliot existed in isolated juxtaposition as the rallying cries of Romanticism and modernism. Such a wish brings with it a vision of a Critical Ode to Mars with two armies, swords out-thrust in eternal stasis, chasing one another beneath massive marble arches inscribed "Be sincerely unconscious" and "Make it New." Indeed, a tiradic critical literature exists, but, as we have seen, the assumption

2 Eliot, *Selected Essays*, 18.
3 Perry Bysshe Shelley, "A Defence of Poetry," in Smith and Parks (eds.), *The Great Critics*, 578–79.

of simple opposition on which it has thrived is falsely conceived.

The passages I have just cited are isolated not only from modifications of other critics but from those of Shelley and Eliot themselves. As for Eliot, we have observed something of the way in which, by his discussion of the objective correlative and by still other comments, he "manages to involve himself," as Brooks and Wimsatt note, "in the language of expressionism." [4] Also, like Shelley, Eliot notes that the mind in creation requires visitation by an invisible influence. Eliot reports that the poet "is haunted by a demon, a demon against which he feels powerless, because in its first manifestation it has no face, no name, nothing; and the words, the poem he makes, are a kind of form of exorcism of this demon." [5]

But if Eliot admits with Shelley that a poem cannot be made until a demon at least pokes the creative coals, so Shelley is not averse to the poet's giving more than one gasp in getting his poem well uttered—or, at least, is not averse to his so arranging mental drafts that the invisible influence can blow more than once on the fading coal of poetic creation. Shelley denies to the poet Eliot's exorcising brew of toil and trouble, but plainly it is to revising or making poems that Shelley refers when he says, "The toil and the delay recommended by critics can be justly interpreted to mean no more than a careful observation of the inspired moments." [6]

In finding Eliot admitting an expressionist influence into his workshop and Shelley carefully observing which way the inspirational breeze is blowing, I scarcely imply that they are saying the same thing. Their greatest critical influence has spread from the extremists' platforms they chose from which to emphasize, respectively, making and expressing. Indeed, we

4 Wimsatt and Brooks, *Literary Criticism*, 668.
5 Quoted in Krieger, *The New Apologists for Poetry*, 55.
6 Shelley, "A Defence of Poetry," 579.

may note with some amusement that if each man entertains an invisible influence, it is in each case a carefully invited presence. Shelley's influence comes like "an inconstant wind" to sail, until it falters, the poet this way or that; Eliot's in diabolic mask challenges: "See if you can make an arrangement of words to get rid of me *this* time." But their provisions for, alternatively, making and expressing are not the less telling for running against the grain of their main designs.

Dramatic theory is not best understood as an Hegelian synthesis of Romantic thesis and impersonal antithesis; but in gathering strands from both doctrines it makes provision for the poet's impulses to expressing and making. From the vantage of dramatic theory's particular accommodation, one may find that which is especially satisfying in both Eliot and Shelley. Considering "the highest kind of criticism" to be the close attention paid by the poet to the poem he is making, surely Eliot is right to say that "some creative writers are superior to others solely because their critical faculty is superior." [7] A thought of that sort restrains the poet's too easy satisfaction with the poem he has wrought by reminding him that he must know what is wrong with his poem if he would have it right. But frequently the poet's identification of what is wrong with his piece does not bring with it an awareness of what would put it right. When that is the case—and I do not insist on it as the only case, for knowledge of right and wrong may come together—the poet can only wait. He will wait patiently but alertly, as a fisherman waits for an unpredictable pull on his lines. That is, quite as Shelley relates, he will observe carefully the inspired moment. It will be the moment at which, the detail to be deleted already recognized, the detail to be inserted floats into his mind.

This example in accommodation of Romantic expression and impersonal making adumbrates dramatic theory of the author's relation to his poem. It is not a negative answer to

[7] Eliot, *Selected Essays*, 18.

the question, "Shouldn't the true poet express what he sincerely feels and say what he means? Or at least try?" Implicit in dramatic doctrine of the speaker is an assumption about the way the true poet tries. Of course he will say what he means in his poem, but in saying a poem he will mean what a poem permits, which is dramatic meaning. A poem will be, for the poet writing it, a form of discourse in which he puts ideas he had before undertaking his poem to dramatic test; or, again, writing his poem will be the poet's means for discovering more fully what his ideas are. If in writing his poem the poet, as Eliot put his case, "does not know what he has to say until he has said it," [8] when he has finished his poem by bringing it to a unified utterance he will have, as Brooks puts it, " 'come to terms' with his experience." [9]

This line of analysis assumes that the poet is a maker of that which is a projection from his own experience; and it concludes, in the fully flourishing dramatic perspective, with a view of the poet as the maker of an implicit speaker expressing his attitudes concerning a matter of interest to himself or, the more usual instance, to some other explicitly or implicitly identified auditor.

The question obviously invited by this statement of dramatic doctrine, in which we consider the poet a maker of that which is a projection of his own experience is: What do we mean by "projection"? The most certain general answer that dramatic theory can give is this: The term implies some modification in the experiences of and attitudes held by the poet before he writes his poem; that is, a modification in relevant data of the poet's biography. We can know neither the modification nor its extent without comparing the poem with the relevant biographical aspects.

The modification may be slight, a selection of salient details, with "projection" in effect meaning "telling selection." George

8 Quoted in Krieger, *The New Apologists for Poetry*, 55.
9 Brooks, *The Well Wrought Urn*, 189.

Barker's "To My Mother" appears to be a characteristic projection of this sort, closely related to life-experience. The speaker explicitly states his love for his mother, a large, brave, hearty, and tender Irishwoman, from whom he is separated in an implicit World War II setting, who cannot be frightened by recurring bombing raids on her city. That is a rough description of content; the poem lies in the vividly particularized quality of the beloved mother's character and personality. As with Owen's "Dulce Et Decorum Est," mentioned above, ordinarily there is little use in our discussing "To My Mother" as the utterance of a speaker. It is George's mother, and we shouldn't want to steal her from him for the sake of a doctrine. Yet, the doctrine of the speaker remains a useful piece of theory, reminding us that Barker's poem selects from all that is Mother—who in some less selective photograph might look merely fat, dumpy and, given her taste for gin, even slightly hung over—details essential to her particular loveliness.

In the case of Owen's poem, I noted contexts in which it could be offensive to speak of the speaker in "Dulce Et Decorum Est"—those would be contexts in which our referring to the poem's speaker might imply that Owen himself, as a British soldier, was not horrified by the combat soldier's life in World War I. Yet again, in so far as the doctrine of the speaker implies modification of the poet's life-experience, it is sound. I note the modification or projection in some discrepancy between Owen's statement in his poem of furious outrage with patriotic slogans and his dying in battle for his country. I am not sure that the word "discrepancy," ambiguous though it is and should be in the context of my present discussion, is properly ambiguous. I would suppose Owen's continuing to fight in British uniform until his death and his protest in "Dulce Et Decorum Est" against jingoistic hypocrisy could be reconciled without difficulty by a knowing biographer. My point is only that which is plainly evident—there is between poet's poem and poet's life a certain disjunction. The poem plainly if indeterminately modifies whatever attitudes were Owen's that permitted him the day before and the day after writing his poem to wake up, kick the rats off his blanket, put on his helmet, and crawl over the top of the trench for another day of the same old grind.

I have been discussing the poem as in some part a modification of relevant or at least tangential biographical aspects in those cases which are least self-evident. Sometimes the fictionalization is obvious, as in Allen Tate's "The Wolves." In this poem the speaker sits in one room while some ill-motivated wolves snuffle and scratch their claws against the floor in the room next door. It is most unlikely that the literal situation was ever endured by Tate or by any other person except, perhaps, some luckless lad who was locked up in a cage at the zoo during a fraternity initiation. But for the speaker in Tate's poem the wolves are real, snarling wolves and the poem is the utterance Tate has made appropriate to a man with such miserable neighbors. Yet we do not for a moment suppose that the poem is unrelated to Tate's own life or that it is other than a projection from some part of his experience and attitudes. I mean more than that we do not doubt it; I mean it is impossible to doubt it. Imagine the slightest measure of involvement possible: that Tate said to himself, "Today I will write a poem," that he then closed his eyes, opened the dictionary, put his finger to the page, opened his eyes, and saw that his finger was placed on the word "wolves." I do not of course insist that his poem began this way. It may be less ludicrous to suppose that he had no stronger immediate impulse to write "The Wolves" than a wish to amplify passages in Webster and Eliot, and perhaps it is less ludicrous still to suppose that Tate's first sense of the poem's design came to him in a flash of anger at being outrageously overcharged for an electric razor. Indeed, with these last examples we are hard on the heels of Eliot's general description of the poet's process of making as the most probable account of

Tate's making "The Wolves." [10] We may rightly suppose that a combination of his experiences (big and little, verbal and silent) and his prevailing attitudes (conscious and unconscious) issued in a poem which utters the words of some poor devil boarded up with a pack of wolves for his fellow lodgers. But, whether we rightly suppose such a combination or ludicrously suppose dictionary word-plucking as the experience and attitudes from which the poem is projected, we must suppose *something*. Even those computers from which fairly decent verse can now be made must be programmed with something before they can whiz out their creations. Hence I shall not argue further that, if a poem of even the most autobiographical sort is in some measure a fiction, it is also true that the most evident fiction—say, *The Tempest*—is projected from experiences and ideas of its author or authors. To argue the latter proposition reduces quickly to the unassailable assertion that fictions must be written by people who are not yet dead—or by computers which have not lost their programs.

As for the author's understanding of the relation of the piece he has written to that in his experience from which it is a projection, there seems to be a wide range of reaction. We have Coleridge's word for it anent "Kubla Khan" that one reaction is, "What am I to think of that?" I can well believe that Owen, finishing "Dulce Et Decorum Est," thought savagely, "Well, at last! I really got said what I really do, after all, think!" And when Frost finished "Provide, Provide" he might have thought, "Did that come out of me?" and he surely

10 Eliot describes this process in *Selected Essays:* "The poet's mind is in fact a receptacle for seizing and storing up numberless feelings, phrases, images, which remain there until all the particles which can unite to form a new compound are present together" (p. 8). Or, again, he says: "When a poet's mind is perfectly equipped for its work, it is constantly amalgamating disparate experience; the ordinary man's experience is chaotic, irregular, fragmentary. The latter falls in love, or reads Spinoza, and these two experiences have nothing to do with each other, or with the noise of the typewriter or the smell of cooking; in the mind of the poet these experiences are always forming new wholes" (p. 247).

thought, on completing some of his poems, "Well, that's a way to look at it." Doubtless free-hand supposition of this sort is an amusement for idle hours. But it is an amusement solidly grounded in likelihood, as our possession of a large number of authors' drafts and revisions strongly suggests. In so far as the piece of literature—whether it be the poem uttered in the first person singular or a Tolstoyan-sized novel with its hundred speakers—is a modification of and projection from interests and experiences in the life of its author, his writing his piece will be for him in some measure an exploration; and the poem he makes for its speaker or speakers to utter will be for him, as author, in some measure a discovery. He may discover little that he did not already know was buried, perhaps, but he will discover something—be it, in relation to the poem as a whole, in general concept or attitude; or, in relation to some detail in the poem, a finer nuance of some perception or idea he only thought he fully possessed. Again, he may discover a great deal. Dylan Thomas hints broadly of extensive discovery when he relates that one of the images from which he makes the poem will "breed" another, and yet another. Thomas discusses his own process of discovery in an imagery of war and peace: "Out of the inevitable conflict of images—inevitable because of the creative, recreative, destructive and contradictory nature of the motivating center, the womb of war—I try to make the momentary peace which is a poem." [11] That is the pleasant sort of extensive discovery. It does not deny the possibility that in writing his fiction the poet may discover more than he wished to know. I do not cite Melville as the certain example, but I should like to know more of his case than I do before deciding otherwise.

As the authorial relation affects the critical biographer, I think we imagine him attending closely the measure and kind of modification effected by the poem in experiences, atti-

[11] Quoted in John L. Sweeney, "Introduction," *Dylan Thomas: Selected Writings* (New York: New Directions, 1946), xv–xvi.

tudes, and ideas of the poet before he wrote his poem. And we should expect from such attention what in some wealth of supply we have from critical biography: reliable accounts of a spectrum of possibilities in modification, depending on the specific author and the specific piece, ranging from dramatic exemplification of known attitudes, through conscious or unconscious preachment to others or himself, to psychic compensation or self-psychotherapy. I think the critical biographer's job must be intrinsically fascinating, work which is never done—at least not until his selected author's most casual thought, personal encounter, note, or letter is publicly revealed.

But, apart from intrinsic interests in the biographer's task, the question of interest to the discourse analyst is what part, if any, the biographical investigation plays in our understanding of poems and their intrinsic meanings. Given a view of the poem as a modification or fictionalization of biographical aspects, the analyst's question is this: Is the modification of such character that the poem's meaning is independent of the poet's biography?

Dramatic theory in its present state of theoretic development will answer in the affirmative. One needs to know nothing of the poet's life to understand that portion of the speaker's life which it is the business of the poetic utterance to reveal; or, briefly, one needs to know nothing of the poet's life to understand the meaning of his poem.

I myself am so thoroughly convinced that we cannot often be led disastrously astray in interpreting a poem's meaning in accord with this limiting implication of dramatic theory that, on reckless days, I am ready to swallow it completely. A view claiming biographical irrelevance has much potential power. Consider again Barker's poem "To My Mother." I have treated the poem as if it were written by a man who loved his mother. But what if we were to learn that the poem was written by a man who had spent his childhood in an orphanage? Surely that would change our sense of what the poem meant to its author. Under those conditions the poem would be his wish fulfillment. Such biographical information almost as surely would change what the poem means to us, as a human document. So, if Barker spent his childhood in an orphanage, it will affect what his "To My Mother" means to him and it will affect what it means to us that a man who was an orphaned child would write a poem like this. But it will not affect the meaning produced in the poem itself: the poem remains the utterance of a speaker addressing his mother, whom he loves as much for her little human foibles as for her gallantry. If Barker's was a motherless childhood, the poem will more drastically modify his life-experience than if he were not an orphan. The poem will be a projection different from the sort it is—just as it would be a projection of still another sort if Barker himself had, as his poem's speaker has, a mother but one whom Barker hated. Whatever the modification, however slight or drastic the projection from related biographical aspects, the poem still means what it intrinsically means as its speaker's unalterable expression of filial love.

So much for one version of dramatic theory as theory, inherently coherent and plainly useful in explaining modifications effected by a poem in its author's biography. Why then, knowing nothing of the biographical facts—and I will assume that you know, as I know, next to nothing of George Barker's life—would we be astonished, and even feel somewhat cheated, to learn that Barker spent an orphaned youth? I am sure that we would be astonished to learn something like that, and that we would be equally astonished to learn, for example, that he wrote his poem shortly after his mother had died from the flu in Boston. Indeed, knowing nothing of his life, we should expect to discover that Barker had a mother, that she was alive when he wrote his poem, that she lived in a bomber-besieged city, and that there was good reason to think that with reasonable consistency he felt for his mother a relatively simple love, uncomplicated by ambiguous relation.

Now, if I am right that we would expect to discover from biographical investigation pretty much what I have just outlined, it will be because we share in the assumption, a perhaps loosely conceived but strongly held assumption nonetheless, of a convention or tradition. The Romantic critic could state the convention clearly, as a point of doctrine: The poem, certainly the poem uttered in the first person singular, is the direct autobiographical expression of its author's feeling, ideas, vision, and the like. I shall assume that, with me, finding Romantic doctrine an inadequate poetics, you have joined the dramatic rebellion. We must leave it to the future to decide whether it was better to be wrong and clear in the bad old Romantic days or to be right and vague in these dramatic times. But the convention, however powerfully it affects our arrangement of betting odds on George Barker's mother, must be put from the perspective of dramatic doctrine, vaguely and even limply, thus: Authorial projections can only go so far.

A vaporous generality, yes; but vapid, no. Or so I think. Indeed, I think its implications, in thorough consideration of dramatic theory, are both interesting and important.

Let me state the two most important implications before explaining them as best I can. First, if authorial projections can go only so far (we have yet to reason together what *that* means), it is not necessarily true that biography is irrelevant to meanings *in* the piece—not true, at least, in the sense that such an assumption provides the best theoretic perspective for our most precise and likely interpretation of a given poem's intrinsic meaning. But, if in saying this we correctly suggest limits in applicability of dramatic doctrine of the speaker, we also, in pointing to that juncture at which meanings in the poem and biographical meanings may interpenetrate, declare dramatic doctrine's value in guiding us to sensitive interpretation. To state the value broadly, dramatic doctrine encourages us to think that the poem may as nicely teach us something about its poet's biography as his biography may teach us something about the meaning effected in the poem.

If we are to understand these implications, we must get a better grip on the convention or tradition which denies unlimited authorial projection from biographical data. The denial does not affect all modes of literature equally. It does not surprise us that, although Macbeth was a murderer, Shakespeare was not, or even that he was not, as in some respects Lady Macbeth was, a woman. And so forth. But it is our expectation that the poem uttered in the first person singular will be its author's highly or intensely personal utterance.

In another context we would want to sort carefully a variety of qualifications. In noting qualifications, we would at once exempt dramatic monologues from our expectation. We would admit the possibility that "The Wolves" may be an admixture of dramatic monologue and symbolistic personal expression, or that, if it is solely the latter, it is surely no more so than Kafka's novel *The Castle*. And we would take account of the fact that a poem may be uttered grammatically in a person other than the first person singular and yet contain within it a psychologically powerful first person thrust or intention. Sensitive readers, noting qualifications like these, remain alert to cues provided within works to right understanding of their fictive measure of projection. Thus, it is our expectation to adjust flexibly to such particularities in fictive limits as may be somehow announced within a given piece of literature. But, qualifications noted, it is our further general expectation that the "I" poem will be intensely personal.

This expectancy is not merely a vestige of nineteenth-century attitudes. True, the Romantic characteristically treated "intensely personal" and "personally intense" as simply convertible terms, when in fact they may mean quite different things. Often enough nineteenth-century poets were tempted by an unnecessarily limited understanding of intensely personal utterance into breast-beating bathos or mewling sentimentality. But to note that condition is, finally, only to refer to bad verse of a certain sort, neither intense nor personal in itself, which nevertheless pays homage, if only with counterfeit coin, to what a lengthy tradition declares that the true poem uttered in the first person singular will be. I do not know how lengthy the tradition is, but I am inclined to say as lengthy as you like—at least long enough to permit our thinking that Sappho's love lyrics were really Sappho's highly personal utterances and that Sappho thought that's what they were too.

Doubtless the tradition does not have an uninterrupted history. For example, the fifteenth-century love lyric "seemed to take . . . poetry farther and farther away from actual human behavior in or out of court." But in reporting this state of affairs, Leonard Nathan reports also the "long-acknowledged poorness of most 15th-century . . . love lyrics" [12] and that it is a "highly limited lyric tradition." [13]

I think it unlikely that dramatic doctrine will be remembered as a theoretic sign of still one more of these disruptive periods. Dramatic doctrine of the speaker may later be regarded—indeed we may so regard it now—as a description of the pains required of a lyric or "I" poet who would utter exactly what he more or less slowly learns he personally really does mean. But nothing in dramatic doctrine, as I at least understand it and would have it understood, declares against our traditional expectancy that the poem uttered in the first

[12] Leonard E. Nathan, "Tradition and Newfangleness in Wyatt's 'They Fle from Me,' " *ELH: A Journal of English Literary History*, XXXII (March 1965) , 8.
[13] *Ibid.*, 1.

person singular will be, when it is completed, an intensely personal utterance.

There is nothing in this line of thought per se which in terms of dramatic doctrine logically forbids our dismissing biographical data for understanding the meaning produced in a poem. Were we to turn, for the intrinsic interest in doing so, to biographical study, we should expect to find a certain compatibility between the poet's lyric or "I" poem and aspects of his biography. But, however personal his utterance, when it finds its completion in the poem, it will be a formed utterance meaning what its speaker says, offering to its reader one general directive for sensitive interpretation: Read it and weep.

I take the view I have just expressed as the strict interpretation of dramatic doctrine in its present stage of development, and I have already stated my belief that it is centrally sound. But it is a view which requires focusing in those cases where there is a large measure of incompatibility between the poem's speaker's apparent meaning and the poem's author's related biographical data. In such cases we must consider the meaning of the poem not only in terms of dramatic doctrine of the speaker, but in the perspective of a long tradition for our expectation that the lyric or "I" poem reflects its author's most personal beliefs and feelings, his personal disposition and regard for things.

We confront such a case, it would seem, in one of William Wordsworth's "Lucy" poems.

> A slumber did my spirit seal;
> I had no human fears:
> She seemed a thing that could not feel
> The touch of earthly years.
> No motion has she now, no force;
> She neither hears nor sees;
> Rolled round in earth's diurnal course,
> With rocks, and stones, and trees.

That is the poem, written in 1799. For the moment I shall not emphasize the sympathy I have with those who find in this poem an image of poor Lucy's dreadful state, rolling through eternity like a zombie, not quite dead perhaps but certainly not alive. Instead I cite the related biographical data, as reported by E. D. Hirsch, Jr.: "Instead of regarding rocks and stones and trees as merely inert objects, [Wordsworth] probably regarded them in 1799 as deeply alive, as part of the immortal life of nature. Physical death he felt to be a return to the source of life, a new kind of participation in nature's 'revolving immortality.' From everything we know of Wordsworth's typical attitudes during which he composed the poem, inconsolability and bitter irony do not belong to the horizon." [14]

To state the broadest limits of a possible incompatibility between the poem's meaning and its author's typical outlook, we would say that in reading Wordsworth's poem we are reading the bitterly unconsoled utterance of a speaker in a poem written by an author in little need of consolation. It is a disparity to make one think. And to make one consider anew an argument like Hirsch's that in order to understand a poem's most probable meaning, we must "posit the author's typical outlook, the typical associations and expectations which form in part the context of his utterance." [15]

Let us then examine the viewpoint suggested by Hirsch, as by biographical critics generally; for, whether or not the poem's meaning must be referred to the poet's typical outlook and, if so, in what manner must surely affect our understanding of rightly expressive intonation of a particular poetic utterance.

14 E. D. Hirsch, Jr., "Objective Interpretation," in Perry (ed.), *Approaches to the Poem*, 100–101.
15 *Ibid.*, 99.

VII

The Poem
as Its Speaker's
Realization of Meaning

$\mathcal{T}$HE reason we have the biographical question with us in theory of poetry is that poems are written by authors. The fact would seem to offer prima facie evidence that they have some sort of vested interest in this business. Consulting their royalty statements, the poets themselves may be inclined to doubt it; and, meeting some of these poets personally, literary critics may be inclined to regret it. But those interesting aspects of the matter lie outside poetics proper, where we admit the unquestionable relationship in order to question its character thus: What is the relation of the poet's personal experiences and outlook, or characteristic attitudes, to the meaning of his poem?

In the present state of analysis of this question the manner—or more precisely the tone—of our answer may well be more useful than the answer we give. I do not suggest that we have had poor analysis of the question, or too little analysis, or even too much. On the contrary, we possess quite penetrating analysis whose results enlarge and clarify our sense of relevant issues. But the question is one of those difficult ones whose most adequate explanation will come—as I think most of us interested in it think it will come—from sorting and relating a variety of insights. I do not mean thereby that on this question polemic is either avoidable or undesirable. Our sorting and relating is accomplished by giving answers to the biographical question, and to give an answer is to take a position. Once critics are in position, the polemical aspect of their common venture is assured. Hence, in my reference to tone of answer I do not deplore positions and polemic or even recommend mild manners—though doubtless civility need not be held against a critic on principle. I mean rather to clarify my own purpose, or the intentional context, in which I shall here discuss three answers, or orders of answer, to the biographical question. In discussing these answers I shall indicate my preference for one of them, thus taking a position. But my purpose is explorative, not annihilative—which demonstrates, I think, my good sense in this matter rather than the goodness of my heart, which is beyond question. Thus, in discussing a variety of answers or lines of explanation, I shall cite a few specific theorists and critics. Further, I seek to preserve a true congruence between what I quote from them and the main thrusts of their arguments and exposition. I do not quote these critics as a hostile force to be put to flight but as persons in charge of some portions of an argument I hold with myself—an argument, it may be said, that modern criticism holds with itself and may be bringing to coherent conclusion.

These introductory remarks will seem scrupulous rather than finical especially to persons knowing the writers to whom I refer, and to many other critics concerned with the biographical question. It is widely understood by theorists that the question is genuinely perplexing, with complex ramifications. Hence, in order to make answer at all, we not only abstract from or reduce others' lines of thought on the matter, but in a real sense we abstract from our own.

I begin with a reduction reasonably innocent of dialectical implication by use of the phrase "typical outlook." The phrase is Professor E. D. Hirsch, Jr.'s. I am not sure that he intends it, or that if he does I would accept it, as entirely equivalent in all contexts to the longer phrase, "the poet's

personal experiences and outlook or characteristic attitudes."
But here I intend it as a rough equivalent, leaving it to
others to worry over unattended ambiguities; or, I mean
more narrowly to refer by the phrase to that part of
the biographical question to which the poet's typical outlook relates. I should like, then, to discuss three answers
or orders of answer to the question of the relation of the
poet's typical outlook to the meaning of his poem: 1) The
poet's typical outlook is irrelevant to the poem's meaning.
2) The poem expresses the poet's typical outlook (or some
aspect of it). 3) The poet's typical outlook is among materials from whose selection the poem's meaning derives.

I can hardly better re-emphasize the exploratory nature
of my intent than by stating my preference for the third
answer, the one nobody understands, although of course I
am working on it. But, besides remarking a difference in
clarity among these answers, or orders of answer, I shall
mention also more noteworthy differences. The first one, in
denying the relevance of the biographical consideration to
theory of poetic meaning, is unlike both of the others. But,
in assuming that the poem's meaning is intrinsic, one and
three are alike and are both different from two. To sum up
these similarities and differences, one and three are alike in
accepting dramatic doctrine of the speaker, but three, the
view that the poet's typical outlook is potential material
for the poem's meaning, is an inclusivist view in that it at-
tempts to accommodate to one, the view that the poet's typical outlook is not relevant to the poem's meanings, the assertion or, as I think of it, the insight of two, that the
poet's typical outlook is relevant.

Assertion of irrelevance of the poet's typical outlook to the
poem's meaning emerges from the theoretic matrix generated
by impersonal theory of poetry. The immediate root of the
assertion of irrevelance is the declaration of the intentional
fallacy. Its discussion by Wimsatt and Beardsley twenty years

ago has exerted such influence that the fallacy may fairly be called, whether in support or refutation, a modern orthodoxy. However, although the Wimsatt and Beardsley position is well known, we may quote their claim as one more reminder of the stakes involved in adequate explanation of the biographical question.

We argue[d] that the design or intention of the author is neither available nor desirable as a standard for judging the success of a work of literary art, and it seems to us that this is a principle which goes deep into some differences in the history of critical attitudes. It is a principle which, accepted or rejected, points to the polar opposites of classical imitation and romantic expression. It entails many specific truths about inspiration, authenticity, biography, literary history and scholarship. . . . There is hardly a problem of literary criticism in which the critic's approach will not be qualified by his view of "intention." [1]

Rejection of the poet's design, or intention to say such-or-such in a poem yet to be written, as a standard for judging the completed poem's artistic success is based on a simple but appealing argument. Wimsatt and Beardsley offer the argument in answer to a rhetorical question, as follows: "One must ask how a critic expects to get an answer about intention. How is he to find out what the poet tried to do? If the poet succeeded in doing it, then the poem itself shows what he was trying to do. And if the poet did not succeed, then the poem is not adequate evidence, and the critic must go outside the poem—for evidence of an intention that did not become effective in the poem." [2]

There is a variety of critical contexts in which this argument may be applauded, amplified, or tested for either limitation or excess of implication. Here I cite it particularly to remark that not so much following from as implicit in this argument is a statement of dramatic doctrine, which Wimsatt

1 W. K. Wimsatt, Jr., and Monroe C. Beardsley, "The Intentional Fallacy," in West (ed.), *Essays in Modern Literary Criticism*, 174–75.
2 *Ibid.*, 175.

and Beardsley put thus: "The meaning of a poem may certainly be a personal one, in the sense that a poem expresses a personality or state of soul rather than a physical object like an apple. But even a short lyric poem is dramatic, the response of a speaker (no matter how universalized). We ought to impute the thoughts and attitudes of the poem immediately to the dramatic *speaker,* and if to the author at all, only by a biographical act of inference." [3]

Doubtless this statement lacks something of semantic and logical elegance. While demonstrating beyond question that a poem is not an apple, Wimsatt and Beardsley leave us in some doubt whether the personality or state of soul that the poem expresses belongs to the poem's speaker or to its author, or somehow to both. Some part of the ambiguity derives from the manner of these critics' assertion that we ought to impute the thoughts and attitudes of the poem to the dramatic speaker. They say that we should impute the poem's thoughts and attitudes "immediately" to the speaker, which may or may not hint that the attitudes should be later or more distantly imputed to the author. If they are to be imputed in due course to the author, then it is contradictory to say that they should not be so imputed except by an act of biographical inference. But, if they are to be imputed solely to the dramatic speaker, it is an imputation patently inapplicable to the meaning of many poems. If, for example, we impute the thoughts and attitudes of all poems to their dramatic speakers, we shall leave the meaning of "My Last Duchess" to the Duke's merciless interpretation.

But of course we know that Wimsatt and Beardsley do not mean to permit any such self-evidently false inference. They will mean, instead, in imputing the thoughts and attitudes of the poem to its dramatic speaker, to refer to a certain sort of poem. The sort of poem to which their comment is certainly intended to apply is that to which they point in reference to the short lyric poem. But in the context of dramatic doctrine—and that of course is the context established by Wimsatt and Beardsley in this statement—the distinguishing characteristic of the sort of poem to which they refer is not that it is short, or even that it sings, as lyrics are sometimes said to sing. The distinguishing characteristic is, rather, that the author of this sort of poem presents himself as its dramatic speaker. This simple fact has a certain appalling impact on Wimsatt's and Beardsley's dramatic doctrine of the speaker; their suggestion that we should impute the thoughts and attitudes of the poem to its dramatic speaker rather than to its author may seem to reduce to the advice that we should impute the poem's attitudes to somebody other than who the dramatic speaker says he is. That would be a remorseless way to understand the old saw that a poet is a liar by profession, and so is his dramatic speaker.

Whether or not Wimsatt and Beardsley offer an entirely precise statement, if I continue in this vein I myself will properly be found ungenerous or simply nagging. I nag against my will, which is to praise this statement by Wimsatt and Beardsley for rendering with complete clarity two important points. First, their statement makes us acutely aware that to explain adequately the relations of a poet's typical outlook to the attitudes in a poem whose speaker is presumably the author himself is by no means a simple task. Second, these critics plainly assert that the poem itself, without our needing to refer further to biographical data, provides data sufficient for its understanding. By the slightest extension, if indeed any extension whatever is required, this assertion of the irrelevance of the poet's biography to poetic meaning may be understood as an assertion that the poet's typical outlook is irrelevant to the poem's meaning. It is a claim which, carrying one dimension of dramatic theory to patiently and even painfully conceived conclusion, deserves our sympathetic attention and appraisal.

Let us look at it, then, while also looking at the diametric view that the poem expresses the poet's typical outlook, in connection with Wordsworth's "A slumber did my spirit seal," quoted earlier.

The bearing of the biographical question on dramatic doctrine is sharply focused by considerations involving Cleanth Brooks's interpretation of this poem's meaning. Brooks treats Wordsworth, as poet, to be the maker of a poem somehow concerned with the "contrast between the speaker's former slumber and the loved one's present slumber." [4] Brooks treats the poem's content as the fictive utterance of an implicit speaker; that is, Brooks does not talk about Wordsworth's attitudes but about those of the lover in the poem. As Professor Hirsch quotes him, Brooks interprets the meaning of Wordsworth's poem as follows:

> [The poet] attempts to suggest something of the lover's agonized shock at the loved one's lack of motion—of his response to her utter and horrible inertness. . . . Part of the effect, of course, resides in the fact that a dead lifelessness is suggested more sharply by an object's being whirled about by something else than by an image of the object in repose. But there are other matters which are at work here: the sense of the girl's falling back into the clutter of things, companioned by things chained like a tree to one particular spot, or by things completely inanimate like rocks and stones. . . . [She] is caught up helplessly into the empty whirl of the earth which measures and makes time in its most powerful and horrible image.[5]

Although Hirsch himself does not approve this interpretation, or the theory which grounds it, as the most reliable possible, he nevertheless states that Brooks's interpretation is "permitted by the text." [6] His reason for judging it permissible is simply this: Brooks states what the poem would mean if someone other than Wordsworth had written it.

[4] Cleanth Brooks, "Irony as a Principle of Structure," 206.
[5] Quoted in Hirsch, "Objective Interpretation," 80–89.
[6] *Ibid.*, 89.

If I barely exaggerate Hirsch's view, and I am not sure that I do, it is with the intent to preserve both his fair and sympathetic statement of reasons for finding the foregoing interpretation of the poem permissible and his own objection to it. Hirsch makes both points as follows:

Now when the *homme moyen sensuel* confronts bereavement such as that which Wordsworth's poem explicitly presents he adumbrates, typically, a horizon including sorrow and inconsolability. These are for him components in the very meaning of bereavement. Sorrow and inconsolability cannot fail to be associated with death when the loved one, formerly so active and alive, is imagined as lying in the earth, helpless, dumb, inert, insentient. And, since there is no hint [in the poem] of life in heaven but only of bodily death, the comforts of Christianity lie beyond the poem's horizon. Affirmations too deep for tears, like those Bateson insists on, simply do not cohere with the poem's text. Brooks's reading, therefore, with its emphasis on inconsolability and bitter irony, is clearly justified not only by the text but by reference to universal attitudes and feelings.

But the trouble with such a reading is apparent to most Wordsworthians. The poet is not an *homme moyen sensuel;* his characteristic attitudes are somewhat pantheistic. Instead of regarding rocks and stones and trees merely as inert objects, he probably regarded them in 1799 as deeply alive, as part of the immortal life of nature. Physical death he felt to be a return to the source of life, a new kind of participation in nature's "revolving immortality." From everything we know of Wordsworth's typical attitudes during the period in which he composed the poem, inconsolability and bitter irony do not belong in its horizon.[7]

This passage vivifies the problems, and in the case of the poem under discussion to the point where they constitute almost a dilemma, in providing an adequate explanation of the poet as both maker and expressionist and of the poem as a highly personal utterance in fictive form. Brooks's is, according to Hirsch, a good analysis of the meaning of the poem, its content understood as the utterance of a context-revealed implicit speaker. But Hirsch also asserts that Wordsworth's

[7] *Ibid.,* 100–101.

typical outlook makes it unlikely that he means in his poem what Brooks finds in it.

Hirsch's emphasis on the importance of an author's characteristic personal outlook to his poem's meaning leads him to advocate Romantic or biographical—or what in a harmless piece of question-begging Hirsch himself calls "Objective"—interpretation as the most reliable method for determining a poet's meaning in his poem. He finds his example in a reading by F. W. Bateson of Wordsworth's poem. According to Hirsch, "since Bateson grounds his interpretation in a conscious construction of the poet's outlook, his reading [in comparison with Brooks's] must be deemed the more probable one until the uncovering of some presently unknown data makes a different construction of the poet's stance appear more valid." [8] That is, in Hirsch's opinion, Bateson's will stand as the more probable reading until possible further biographical research turns up evidence qualifying our present sense of Wordsworth's characteristic attitudes.

In Bateson's reading, Wordsworth's poem illustrates and reaffirms his typical outlook. Bateson offers the Romantic or biographical interpretation of the poem we have read above, as follows:

The final impression the poem leaves is not of two contrasting moods, but of a single mood mounting to a climax in the pantheistic magnificence of the last two lines. . . . The vague living-Lucy of this poem is opposed to the grander dead-Lucy who has become involved in the sublime processes of nature. We put the poem down satisfied, because its last two lines succeed in effecting a reconciliation between the two philosophies or social attitudes. Lucy is actually more alive now that she is dead, because she is now a part of the life of Nature, and not just a human "thing!" [9]

Professor Hirsch, while approving biographical interpretation from which Bateson's reading derives, nevertheless quali-

8 *Ibid.,* 101.
9 Quoted in *Ibid.,* 89.

fies it. Although Bateson's method is "fundamentally sound," it remains possible that his interpretation of this particular poem may be wrong because "a poet's typical attitudes do not always apply to a particular poem." [10] Hirsch offers his qualification in behalf of good sense. Without it the argument for the biographical method would become impossibly circular, meaning little more than this: a reading like Bateson's is permissible because it squares neatly with Wordsworth's typical outlook, but Wordsworth's typical outlook is largely established on the basis of permissible readings, like Bateson's, of Wordsworth's poems.

But admission of the possibility of atypicality all the more clearly invites our attention to the inherent difficulty in biographical interpretation. Simply, there is nothing in our knowledge of a poet's typical outlook to tell us in itself whether or not a particular poem is atypical or in what respect it is atypical. Our best and possibly our sole source for a judgment of that sort must lie in the content of the poem itself. I believe there is no serious alternative to this assumption which would permit our identification of a given poem's meaning as atypical of its author's characteristic attitudes. Hence, we cannot on the basis of knowledge of Wordsworth's typical outlook automatically approve Bateson's reading for finding Wordsworth's typical outlook expressed in his poem. Instead, we must read Wordsworth's piece to discover if Bateson is right in thinking that Wordsworth's typical outlook applies to this particular poem.

Acceptance of this analysis of the methodological limitation of biographical criticism might seem to leave us no alternative but to return to the method, indifferent to biographical consideration, proposed by Wimsatt and Beardsley, which apparently grounds Brooks's reading of Wordsworth's poem. But I do not believe this to be our necessary or best interpretive recourse, though the alternative I think proper remains a dra-

[10] *Ibid.*, 101.

matic theory of interpretation. Instead of denying the biographical claim, continuing its analysis along the line established above helps us understand better the nature of the claim that can responsibly be made. The valid claim, broadly put, is that a possible or even highly likely component of poetic utterance is the poet's characteristic attitude or typical outlook, or some part of his outlook; that is, his typical outlook is material which may comprise, though in unpredictable ways and measure, some part of his poem's meaning.

To amplify briefly, I have said that we may learn from a given poem that it is atypical of the poet's characteristic outlook. That authorizes the poem rather than the poet's biography to declare an atypical meaning or outlook. But if his poem itself may declare an atypical meaning, obviously his poem may also declare a typical meaning. Indeed, in the sort of poem we are particularly considering—that is, the lyric poem or, more exactly described in the perspective of dramatic doctrine, the poem in which the author presents himself as the dramatic speaker—the likelihood is that our best if not sole source, and quite possibly also the poet's best source, for discovering his typical outlook is from reading his poetry.

This assertion requires explanation of the sources and character of a poet's typical outlook. There are two general sources for discovering the typical outlook of an author—his work and the visible aspects of his life exclusive of his work. By "visible" I mean simply whatever can be found out about him—the society and time in which he lived, whom and what he loved and hated and why, whom he met and what they did and what they said to one another. I add, to no particular theoretic point except that which would, in some context other than this one, test the biographer's claim as critic of a man's life, that if we really mean by an author's "life" his life I personally doubt that much of it is visible; if this is true, the most diligent and discerning biographer actually draws his conclusions about the author's life from a miserable assortment of visible bits and snatches. Whatever may be the truth of that matter, we conventionally refer these visibilities to "the man," thus speaking of the man and his work, or the man and the author, or the poet and his life. The distinction between man and work affords the possibility of an interesting variety of simply harmonious or contrapuntal relations, even to the point of outright division where we might conclude that the work's typical outlook contradicts—as psychic compensation or self-persuasion of some sort or another—the typical outlook of the man.

But, in the piece in which he presents himself as the dramatic speaker, the author accepts as part of the terms that he will not foreknowingly contradict his typical outlook as a man. The reservation I intend in the qualifying word "foreknowingly" is this: I mean that the author of the "I" poem—though he assumes his own outlook, as man, as his dramatic speaker's outlook—is not thereby committed before the writing of each new piece to consult his typical outlook to see what he should say next. Indeed, the poet—for a long time, at least, in his career as poet—may not know what his typical outlook is. He may only slowly discover his typical outlook by writing his poems, as his readers discover it by reading them. That is why we like to see an "I" poet well along in years and with many poems behind him before we speak with confidence of his typical outlook, and we are only entirely confident of his typical outlook when he has entirely made, as we say, the crossing of the bar.

Given this view, according to which we understand that in discussing a poet's typical outlook we are discussing that which significantly derives from the collective, or collecting, content and meaning of his separate poems, we are better able to evaluate the strengths and shortcomings of that dramatic theory of interpretation which would forego the biographical consideration as simply irrelevant to the meaning of the poem. John Perry, urging the method for our interpretation of Wordsworth's poem, argues that the poem's meaning may be determined by considering the poem a "self-limited verbal context," by which phrase Perry plainly means certain words in a certain order which might have been written by an anonymous author of this and no other poem.[11] The value of this view is considerable and evident. Taking that view, we shall not guess before we read the poem what it means; and upon reading it we shall assume that it means what its implicitly revealed speaker thinks it means, because it is the kind of poem whose author will think it means, or ought to mean, that. But in the perspective of our foregoing discussion the weakness of Perry's recommended method of interpretation is equally evident. The weakness is simply stated. Analysis like Perry's unnecessarily limits the relevant verbal context in which the poem's meaning may be determined. The more reliable and larger context is, roughly, the poet's works as a whole.

The meanings a poet activates or releases in a given poem derive from two potential sources—conventional or dictionary meanings of words used in the poem and such special meanings of words as the poet has already activated in other of his poems. In saying this, far from intending anything either novel or complex, I mean but to reassert a commonplace in the experience of the reader, who may come better to understand nuances of meanings in a given poem by a given poet through reading a large number or all of his poems. This report of a general experience in reading is by no means translatable into a rule that all of a poet's works must be read before any one of them may be understood. I submit merely that as a poet's works activate or release characteristically personal meanings and attitudes, or his typical outlook, then characteristically personal meanings become part of the verbal or material matrix from which he makes still more poems and their meanings. How much the context of his poetry as a whole, or

11 Perry, "Analysis and Interpretation of Poems by Varied Means," 14.

some part of his whole poetry, contributes to meanings in a particular poem depends on both the poem and the poet being read. Critical judgment of the exact specification will be a matter of decision.

Dramatic doctrine implies that our decision in the matter is best derived from treatment of the poem as its speaker's cohering utterance. In identifying the intentional fallacy, Wimsatt and Beardsley suggest that "poetry is a feat of style by which a complex of meaning is handled all at once. Poetry succeeds because all or most of what is said or implied is relevant; what is irrelevant has been excluded, like lumps from pudding and 'bugs' from machinery." [12] We are well agreed that what is said in a poem is relevant; thus, we expect it to be relevant *to* something. Dramatic doctrine, in treatment of the poem as its speaker's cohering utterance, suggests the relevance: What the poem says is relevant to what the poem's implicit speaker means. The words in a given poem may or may not release meanings expressed elsewhere in the poet's works. Alert to the possibility, we determine whether or not it is actualized by analyzing how the particular utterance which is the particular poem coheres.

Treatment of the words in the poem as its speaker's cohering utterance does not afford automatic understanding of his meaning. I personally am grateful for this. I should dislike a theory which suppressed discussion of individual poems. But to consider the poem as its speaker's cohering utterance is to put freedom of its discussion under the rule of law. It may even help us be self-critical as we ask ourselves: If the speaker of this poem means what I think he means, would he say what he says here? That is a question to gladden the heart of a poet; it encourages his readers to read his poem more than once.

We may observe something of the effect of considering the poem as its speaker's cohering utterance by suggestive anal-

12 Wimsatt and Beardsley, "The Intentional Fallacy," 176.

ysis of Brooks's and Bateson's reading of the Wordsworth poem which we have been considering. My intention is not to prove two readings wrong in order to produce triumphantly a third right reading which would be, naturally enough, my own. I do not even mean to explore the critiques mentioned exhaustively or at length. But I hope to suggest that to understand the poem as its speaker's cohering utterance provides a reliable context for our discussion of what he means in saying what he says.

Let us place first in this interpretive perspective Bateson's reading as that most ready to find the speaker of the poem meaning Wordsworth's typical outlook. According to Bateson, the poem's speaker means that Lucy, by dying, rather improves her position. That is, "Lucy is actually more alive now that she is dead, because she is now a part of the life of Nature, and not just a human 'thing.' " In accord with treatment of the poem as its speaker's cohering utterance, our interpretive question is simply this: Would a speaker intending such a meaning say the poetic text? To ask the question is to attend in a somewhat different and perhaps more rewarding perspective Hirsch's noting "the apparent implausibility of Bateson's reading." [13] Hirsch means that in the context of ordinary attitudes it seems implausible for the poem's speaker to mean what Bateson finds him to mean, but that nevertheless Bateson's reading is probable because it is consonant with Wordsworth's typical outlook. But here we assume Wordsworth's typical outlook—rather optimistically pantheistic, full of awed delight in what Bateson terms "the sublime processes of nature"—as material which may play a part in a poem in which Wordsworth presents himself as dramatic speaker. We assume, further, that if the poem's speaker means to express Wordsworth's typical outlook, he will mean what Bateson says he means. Treatment of the poem as its speaker's cohering utterance does not require us to deny these assump-

13 Hirsch, "Objective Interpretation," 101.

tions. Rather, it requires us to ask this: Would a speaker meaning what Bateson thinks he means say what he says? There would appear to be a few good reasons to doubt it. Hirsch, though generally approving the reading, offers some of the reasons in noting that Bateson "fails to emphasize properly the negative implications in the poem ('No motion has she now, no force')" and that "he overlooks the poet's reticence, his distinct unwillingness to express any unqualified evaluation of his experience." [14] I can only think it would have greatly affected Hirsch's sense of what both Wordsworth and Bateson were up to had he considered not the poet's but the speaker's reticence. I briefly interpolate this remark in citing Hirsch's judgment of failures he finds in Bateson. Although the latter's reading is, according to Hirsch, more probable than Brooks's, nevertheless "Bateson overstates his case." [15] But in the context in which we are now viewing his reading, whatever may be Bateson's failures, they do not derive from overstatement of his case. They derive instead from his lucid and consistent presentation of it. He leaves us in no doubt of Wordsworth's typical outlook. In remarking failures in Bateson's reading, Hirsch is really reminding us that a speaker who means what Bateson finds this poem's speaker to mean should say something different.

I have said that Bateson does not overstate his case for the biographical interpretation. In an important particular he understates it. In Bateson's interpretation it is of crucial importance that the poem's speaker means that Lucy, in dying into incorporation with sublime natural process, is thereby exalted in character from mere human "thing-"hood. But, in Wordsworth's poem "Lucy Gray," little Lucy is characterized as "The sweetest thing that ever grew/Beside a human door." That sweet thing gives us some reason to suppose that, although the word "thing" carries no air of distinction for Mr.

14 *Ibid.*
15 *Ibid.*

Bateson, the dictionary, or you and me, Wordsworth was pressing or trying to press something rather pantheistic out of it. That sweetest thing growing beside the door is certainly not subhuman, but it is not merely human either. It is a particularly precious bundle of natural process, growing— how? Like a flower, like a shrub, in any event like other natural spontaneities of the pantheist proclamation. I shall follow this special thing no farther down the interpretive tunnel, but we have gone far enough to see that it leads to some part of Wordsworth's typical outlook.

Lucy's thinginess and what it does or does not mean, given its use in this and other of Wordsworth's poems, also bears significantly on Brooks's reading of "A slumber did my spirit seal." Brooks finds the speaker to mean that Lucy's is a horrible death, a falling back "into the clutter of things." But since, before dying, she seemed a thing that could not feel the touch of earthly years, it would appear that whatever else may be said of Lucy's fate, in falling back into the clutter of things she did not have very far to fall. Now if the speaker means by "thing" just any old thing, he will have chosen a miserable way to speak of her preciousness to him in life. But if in the Wordsworthian verbal matrix "thing" hints of something preciously spiritual-natural, Lucy will then be joining other precious things, such as rocks and trees, in falling back among them. How precious is the clutter of things? It may be the question the speaker means almost to ask in saying this poem. Brooks, finding the speaker of the poem in a state of "agonized shock," touches on a point which suggests the possibility that the speaker himself is having some second thoughts concerning Wordsworth's typical regard for rocks and stones. Brooks comments on the line, "I had no human fears," that the "human fears" are apparently "the fears normal to human beings" but that developments in the poem "warp the phrase" in the direction of "fears *for* the loved one as a mortal human being." [16] But there is a still

16 Brooks, "Irony as a Principle of Structure," 205.

more inclusive possibility. If the speaker's fears depend and turn on this loved girl's fate, they may also include a more comprehensive fear for the human condition generally. This reading would find the poem's speaker meaning that, given his sense of sublime natural process, he had not worried about man's mortality until Lucy's death so struck him with grief that even he, though fully committed to Wordsworth's typical outlook, could tell the difference between Lucy and a rock. And I do not intend a pointless, coarse joke. For a man of somewhat pantheistic disposition, convinced of the sublimity of nature's processes, to be abruptly jolted by one of them would refer his self-declared "slumber" not only to his painfully disproven assumption that Lucy could not die but to his general sense of nature's processes in their relation to man. I do not assert that the speaker is recanting his author's views, which will be his own. Rather I mean that, once one assumes that Wordsworth's typical outlook represents possible or even likely material for this poem's particulars, they suggest that he means that rocks, stones, and trees are not, in the moment of his utterance, giving him his customary sense of satisfaction in their being.

These few remarks hardly comprise a convincing interpretation of Wordsworth's poem, but they may suggest the frame of reference in which we may expect to read the poem most reliably. In his essay to which I have been referring, Professor Hirsch says rightly that "interpretation is the construction of *another's* meaning." I would apply his comment to effect a certain modification in his conclusion that "A slight shift in the way we speak about texts would be highly salutary. It is natural to speak not of what a text says, but of what an author means." [17] Hirsch's emphasis usefully reminds us that if we confine ourselves to referring to what a text says we must conclude simply, unless we are ready to pledge our faith in the heresy of paraphrase, that the text says what the text says. But, as for what is meant by what the text says,

[17] Hirsh, "Objective Interpretation," 106.

the author of a poem means what his poem's implied speaker means. Supposing the speaker, like speakers of other kinds of discourse, to mean something, we must find his meaning as it emerges from his cohering utterance which comprises the poetic text. We should enjoy that way of regarding a poem of the personal sort, as we hear it spoken by a speaker who says what he means and means what he says.

It may take us awhile in reading what the speaker says to find out what he means. Only rarely will he mean not to know what he means. J. Alfred Prufrock is probably in this condition; anyhow, Eliot put him in a dramatic monologue for punishment. Of course, even if the speaker broadly hints that he would like to mean something, if the author who makes what the speaker says is maladroit, we may never find out what he means. In any event, it may take the good author awhile, as he makes the cohering utterance of his speaker, to find out what his speaker means.

Probably we are right to suppose that the author of the lyric or "I" poem, in finding out what the speakers of his poems mean, is also discovering what he, the author, means. In this connection I note that in a poem written a few years prior to "A slumber did my spirit seal" Wordsworth stated at least once quite baldly, and as if he did not know at all what his typical outlook was supposed to be, the "perilous weakness" in entrusting to nature "a happy end of all." [18] I draw from this evidence the conclusion that Wordsworth was not a typical outlook but a man, and that his typical outlook emerged from engagement in the data of his own existence. It should not surprise us that in writing his poems the poet may discover, and in the case of some poets perhaps only slowly discover, rather than steadily express a pre-formed, monistic typical outlook.

The content of poems strongly suggests that exploration of experience is central to the poet's enterprise. His poem not

[18] In "Vaudracour and Julia."

only tells us what he discovered but represents the process of discovery. When we speak of a poem's meaning—in the case of the lyric or "I" poem, its speaker's meaning—I think we are stating what we think it is that, in saying what he says in the poem, the speaker reports himself to be discovering. Let my preliminary example be drawn from critiques, already briefly considered, of Wordsworth's poem. Brooks interprets the speaker of Wordsworth's poem to realize that Lucy's death is horrible. Bateson interprets the speaker to realize that Lucy's death is magnificent. I toyed with a further possibility that the speaker realizes that his pantheistic *weltanschaung* must be taken back to the drawing board. These three readings comprise a fair paradigm of variety in the interpretive assault on the meaning of a poem. But they also represent another paradigm of, I think, more consequential interest. Although the readings differ in what they find the poem's speaker to be realizing, they all find him to be realizing *something*.

I would have my example prepare for a conclusion something like this. The poetic text is what its speaker says. In saying what he says, he reports himself discovering or realizing something that he did not know to be the case until he realized it. What he realizes is what, in saying the words in their order which is the poem, he means. When we ask about the speaker, "What does he mean?" we are asking, "What, saying what the text says, does its speaker realize or come to realize?" A way of putting this is to refer to discovery or realization as a poem's structural principle. Let us next so consider it.

VIII | The Speaker's Realization as Appraisive Conclusion

I do not think of dramatic theory as a fully articulated account of poetic discourse but as an analytic investigation still in progress. Doubtless we cannot entirely gauge the potential for development in poetics which may derive from attention to, as Brooks and Warren refer to it, the "dramatic aspect of poetry." But we may well find stimulating their more complete comment: "In reading poetry it is well to remember this dramatic aspect and to be sure that one sees the part it plays in any given poem." [1] Dramatic doctrine as continuing analysis simply takes this statement seriously; indeed, it is well to remember the dramatic aspect—the problem is to determine what part it plays.

That is a question to be put to the particular case of "any given poem." It is also a question which, put to various poetic species, may affect our general expectations concerning the nature of poetic content; Brooks himself suggests that we may think of the poem as a structure of attitudes. Still another general expectancy afforded by dramatic analysis is that the poem's speaker realizes a significance or meaning. That is, in thinking of the poem as representing, as Brooks and Warren suggest, the reaction of its speaker, we may observe that his reaction is frequently or even customarily to realize something. Of conventional or dictionary meanings of

1 Brooks and Warren, *Understanding Poetry*, 23.

the word "realize" I refer particularly to its meaning "to conceive vividly as real; as, he *realized* his danger." Thus, in "A slumber did my spirit seal," Wordsworth realizes that, in having assumed nature's steady beneficence and good will toward men, he was dreaming. My point of course is not to fight against all comers for this interpretation of what Wordsworth realizes; we have already observed differing conclusions among specific readings of the poem. But the interpretive variety turns on a shared assumption that the speaker realizes *something*.

I have suggested that we may think of the speaker's characteristic realization of significance as a structural principle of the poem. Doubtless more than one structural principle is at work in a given poem; for example, a simple formal structural principle of the sonnet is that it shall consist of fourteen lines. In so far as the speaker's realization of significance is a structural principle, it affects our understanding of a poem's meaning, what it "says."

Elder Olson, in his discussion of Yeats's "Sailing to Byzantium" in "Prolegomena to a Poetics of the Lyric," approaches treatment of the speaker's realization as a structural principle of meaning. Olson's own emphasis is on showing Yeats's poem, as an example of one kind of lyric poem, as a "dialectical argument through the logic of images." [2] But

2 This is Perry's accurate summary description in "Analysis and Interpretation of Poems by Varied Means," of Elder Olson, " 'Sailing to Byzantium': Prolegomena to a Poetics of the Lyric," in Perry (ed.), *Approaches to the Poem*, 181–95. Olson's paper was first published in *University Review* in 1942. When, a few years later, Olson returned to consideration of this poem in another context—see Elder Olson, "An Outline of Poetic Theory," in Crane (ed.), *Critics and Criticism*, 546–66—his analysis of Yeats's poem is more explicitly dramatic. In "Prolegomena," for example, Olson suggests that "since there is no action" in the poem "there is no agent, that is *character*, in the sense in which there are differentiated agents in drama or epic . . . ; rather, the character in the sense in which character may be said to exist here is almost completely universalized" (p. 193). But on reconsideration, in "An Outline," Olson determines the character to be in effect the dramatic speaker: "We may illustrate the nature of a special poetics a little further by outlining

a major aspect of Olson's critique might be referred more accurately to the speaker's revaluation of objects of his interest declared within the poem, and Olson so refers it. That is, he notes several "terms, one might say, from which the poem suspends: the condition of the young, who are spiritually passive although sensually active; the condition of the merely old, who are spiritually and physically impotent; the condition of the old, who, although physically impotent, are capable of spiritual activity; the condition of art considered as inanimate—i.e., the condition of things which are merely monuments; and finally the condition of art considered as animate—as of such things as artificial birds which have a human soul." [3] Concerning these central aspects of the poem's content, Olson reports provocatively, "About these several oppositions the poem forms. The whole turns on the old man's realization, now that he is in the presence of the images of Byzantium, that these images have souls." The speaker's realization in this particular poem has the effect, as Olson observes, of dividing it into two major parts, its "first two stanzas presenting art as inanimate, the second two, as animate." Thus, in the first two stanzas of the four-stanza poem, in which the speaker regards the art objects or images as "merely objects of contemplation, they may be neglected or studied, visited or not visited," but "in stanzas III and IV they are treated as gods which can be prayed to for life or death, as beings capable of motion from sphere to sphere, as in-

---

briefly that of the species to which Yeats's 'Sailing to Byzantium' belongs. It is a species which imitates a serious action of the first order mentioned above, i.e., one involving a single character in a closed situation, and the character is not simply in passion, nor is he acting upon another character, but has performed an act actualizing and instancing his moral character, that is, has made a moral choice. It is dramatic in manner— the character speaks in his own person . . ." (pp. 563–64). Olson's comments in "An Outline," while not contradicting his analysis in "Prolegomena," clarify and more lucidly present the earlier piece's dramatic implications.

3 Olson, "Prolegomena," 185–86.

structors of the soul, as sages possessed of wisdom." [4] In short, the speaker's realization is not only that the images have souls but that they can instruct his own soul to its brilliant if self-evidently unnatural consummation, in immortal triumph over natural decay and death, as he foresees himself formed "Of hammered gold and gold enammeling" and "set upon a golden bough to sing / To lords and ladies of Byzantium / Of what is past, or passing, or to come." His approaching or possible immortality is what the speaker realizes, and, in saying the words which are the poem, that which he realizes is that which he means.

Consideration of the speaker's realization as his meaning provides an interesting perspective in which to review central features of what Cleanth Brooks called in 1947, in a phrase quickly to receive widespread currency, "the heresy of paraphrase." Brooks did not argue against the value of paraphrase per se, but against its being based on conceiving of the poem as its logical précis suffused with emotion. As he wrote, "We can very properly use paraphrases as pointers and as short-hand references provided that we know what we are doing and that we see plainly that the paraphrase is not the real core of meaning which constitutes the essence of the poem." [5] In offering this cautionary comment on paraphrasing, Brooks well understood both the difficulty for us in analysis if we are not to look for a core of meaning and the psychological appeal of views according to which "the poem constitutes a 'statement' of some sort, the statement being true or false, and expressed more or less clearly or eloquently or beautifully." [6] As Brooks put it, "We tend to embrace the doctrine of a logical structure the more readily because, to many of us, the failure to do so seems to leave the meaning of the poem hopelessly up in the air. The alternative possi-

4 *Ibid.*, 186.
5 Brooks, *The Well Wrought Urn*, 181.
6 *Ibid.*, 179.

bility will appear to us to lack even the relative stability of an Ivory Tower: it is rather commitment to a free balloon. For to deny the possibility of pinning down what the poem 'says' to some 'statement' will seem to assert that the poem really says nothing." [7]

As we know, Brooks provides his own "positive account of what a poem is and does," emphasizing particularly under the subsuming rubric of "Irony" the organic relations of a poem's parts.[8] A number of Brooks's speculations have encouraged us to think of poetic content and meaning in a dramatic perspective. In so viewing the poem, I think we may often find it useful to consider the poem's meaning in relation to its speaker's realization of significance. If this truly is a useful way to consider the poem, it suggests an immediately rewarding analytic alternative to that implied by the paraphrastic heresy, about which Brooks concludes: "one may sum up by saying that most of the distempers of criticism come about from yielding to the temptation to take certain remarks which we make *about* the poem—statements about what it says or about what truth it gives or about what formulations it illustrates—for the essential core of the poem itself." [9] As Brooks puts the matter, he is surely right. But if we alter this passage somewhat, changing "poem" to "speaker" and "it" to "he," we will deliver a curiously dissatisfying opinion: "one may sum up by saying that most of the distempers of criticism come about from yielding to the temptation to take certain remarks which we make about the speaker—statements about what he says or about what he thinks to be true or about what formulations he would illustrate—for the essential core of his meaning itself." Of course this is an unsatisfying warning, and there is much in Brooks's writings to suggest that he would find it dissatisfying, too. Still, I think we may take a certain naughty delight from this statement

[7] *Ibid.*, 185.
[8] See Brooks, "Irony as a Principle of Structure," especially pp. 196–200.
[9] Brooks, *The Well Wrought Urn*, 182.

which, simply because it is so unconvincing, suggests a temptation to state in our own words the poem's meaning, to which we may decorously yield. Nor will we, in yielding, reintroduce the treacherous paraphrastic heresy. That is, if the speaker realizes something in saying the words which are the poem, he realizes what he does because the words in their order in the poem are what they are and not something else. But if, in saying the poem, the speaker realizes something, we honor him in observing what it is. Also, we may put his realization quite well in our own words, even though we speak prose. Further, if the speaker's realization, which we find by reading his words in the poem and announce in our own words in our explication, is what he means in saying the poem, we must attend still another likelihood: If the speaker's realization is what he means, in the case of the lyric or "I" poem what its speaker means can be reasonably understood to be what the poem itself means. The poem says what it and nothing else says, but it means what its speaker realizes. We may thrash about at great length critically discussing in our own words what his realization is. We not only properly *may* do this; in fact, we do it.

As this observation and my previous remarks bear on the theory of analysis or practical criticism, they plainly apply to our discussion of the poem's theme. In *Understanding Poetry,* Brooks and Warren define theme as "the basic idea or attitude which is presented in a poem." [10] This is a good as well as conventional definition which—when guarded by proper cautions that the poem is more than its theme—we shall find in a variety of educative contexts continually useful. The effect of considering the speaker's realization as a structural principle is not to prevent our looking for the poem's basic idea but to suggest something of the nature of the basic idea we are likely to find. As this comment relates to the sort of questions we pose in the classroom, I suppose a variety of

10 P. 695 (Revised edition, 1951).

occasions in which, instead of asking "What is the poem's basic idea or attitude?," we will find it more productive to ask, "What does the speaker realize?"

That question, or a variant of it, implies our assuming the likelihood that the lyric or "I" poem's theme or basic idea turns on a contrastive state of some sort and measure, designated within the poem and which from the point of view of the poem's speaker represents his realization of significance. That is, the poem records the process of the speaker's realization.

Wordsworth's "A slumber did my spirit seal" and Yeats's "Sailing to Byzantium" can be taken as examples of the sort of poem in which the speaker's realization is shown or represented in the poem itself. In Wordsworth's poem it is less explicit than in Yeats's poem. Probably it is also less certain, by which I mean not so much that we cannot certainly say what Wordsworth's speaker realizes (though that, too, may be the case) as that Wordsworth's speaker is probably not altogether certain of what he realizes—though, as I would have it, he realizes that he is uncertain. The range of possibility in both the explicitness and definiteness of speakers' realizations is wide indeed, and we judge these matters not by a general rule but by analysis of particular poems. In a given poem explicitly stated realizations may be affected by implicit realizations which are equally or more important to our understanding what the poem's speaker comprehensively realizes in saying the words which are his poem.

Let us notice the effect in a familiar poem, Matthew Arnold's "Dover Beach." As you recall, the speaker, who bears a striking resemblance to Matthew Arnold, is enjoying the night air beside a window overlooking the English coast as he begins to speak, somewhat to himself and somewhat to the woman he loves, who is near him in the room:

> The sea is calm tonight;
> The tide is full, the moon lies fair

Upon the straits;—on the French coast the light
Gleams and is gone; the cliffs of England stand,
Glimmering and vast, out in the tranquil bay.
Come to the window, sweet is the night-air!
Only, from the long line of spray
Where the sea meets the moon-blanched land,
Listen! you hear the grating roar
Of pebbles which the waves draw back, and fling,
At their return, up the high strand,
Begin, and cease, and then again begin,
With tremulous cadence slow, and bring
The eternal note of sadness in.

Sophocles long ago
Heard it on the Aegean, and it brought
Into his mind the turbid ebb and flow
Of human misery; we
Find also in the sound a thought,
Hearing it by this distant northern sea.

The Sea of Faith
Was once, too, at the full, and round earth's shore
Lay like the folds of a bright girdle furled.
But now I only hear
Its melancholy, long, withdrawing roar,
Retreating, to the breath
Of the night-wind, down the vast edges drear
And naked shingles of the world.

Ah, love, let us be true
To one another! for the world, which seems
To lie before us like a land of dreams,
So various, so beautiful, so new,
Hath really neither joy, nor love, nor light,
Nor certitude, nor peace, nor help for pain;
And we are here as on a darkling plain
Swept with confused alarms of struggle and flight,
Where ignorant armies clash by night.

So there we have it: the thinking man's love poem. I am
tempted, before saying a word about what *he* says, to deplore
the speaker as a man who does not know when he is well off.

As he himself notes, since the time of Sophocles—that is, from time immemorial—the more deeply a man thinks on the nature of life, the more miserably he realizes what a miserable mess he has on his hands. And knowing that—indeed, announcing that—here is the speaker, for the moment with no drafty school to inspect or deadly dull lecture-writing chore to perform, but far from the crowd in his little enclave by the sea on a beautiful night, his loved one within arm's reach, and what does he do? He reflects. O Adam, O Eve, how could you have done this to us?—thus leaving us forever unfulfilled in our desire for the simple life, our desire to loll nakedly in the lily-patch, and from time to time look up in perfect silence at the stars, while we sip a little mango juice. Well, after all, meaning to express annoyance with it, I but offer a thin, distorting echo of Arnold's mighty moan, and I must leave off for his sake as well as to get back to structural business.

Although we find "Dover Beach" a reflective, melancholy, and even anguished utterance, it is not a poem which we think of as hard or intricate, with deeply submerged meanings. The speaker leaves us in little doubt of the contrast he finds between the world's lovely, tempting appearance and its bitter reality. Explicitly he states the world's comfortless reality in a remorseless listing of its inexhaustible negations of our desires and needs. Surely this is a grim realization, but deeply involved in it is another powerful and even dominant, though largely implicit, realization. In tortured awareness of the world's hostile indifference, the speaker realizes—in the sense of both intensified recognition and discovery—his loved one's preciousness; he realizes his desperate need for her love and their mutually crucial need to be true to, to love and support, one another. Thus his rather illogical suggestion that he and another must and can love one another in a world in which there is no love is nevertheless his best possible psychological resolution of his crisis in awareness.

The effect of the poem's final figure of clashing armies tells us much of the interrelations between the speaker's love of a person and his dismal sense of the world in which they live. None of us doubts the figure's power, nor need we look far for its cause. Coleridge would have termed it a figure of imagination rather than fancy; we refer to it as a metaphor whose meanings are internal.[11] That is, the figure does not merely illustrate or dramatize the concept of a terrifying world, although it does do that vividly. The juxtaposed realizations of personal need and horrific world are here, in the final figure, collected and fused in a fierce and piteous image—as the speaker realizes that he and his loved one can count on nothing but their own personal relation for such consolation and fragile, incessantly imperiled, security as they may find.

As the example of "Dover Beach" makes clear, the poem's speaker's realization represents an evaluative or appraisive conclusion. As a critique of Arnold's speaker's meaning, my few remarks leave unattended some consequential matters. For example, by a process of tenuous association best understood by the person of moralizing disposition, the movement of the sea-tide beyond his window reminds the speaker of the contrast between the faithful past and the faithless present. Some readers have followed this contrast, explicitly emphasized in the poem and supported by implications released into the poem by Arnold's writings as social critic, to discover in the final figure an image of the effects of late nineteenth-century capitalism, or at least late nineteenth-century British

11 Krieger succinctly summarizes this aspect of I. A. Richards' thought-provoking discussion—see Richards, *Coleridge on Imagination*, especially pp. 72–79—in *The New Apologists for Poetry:* "Coleridge's distinction between imagination and fancy becomes for Richards an analysis of tenor-vehicle relationships in the metaphor. The imagination is displayed in an image which is internal and functional, the organizing principle of the passage; a passage is produced only by fancy if the image is merely external, accidental, decorative. In fancy the tenor and vehicle are always distinct; in imagination the tenor is fused into its vehicle" (p. 62).

society, on the individual expectation. Again, Arnold's comparing the "human misery" of which he speaks to that which Sophocles well knew suggests its reference to a recurringly general human condition rather than merely to one social condition or disorder. I do not doubt that one or the other, or probably both, of these realizations of significance are, within the poem, enfolded to one or another effect in the dominating or subsuming realization of Arnold's conclusion. Interpreters can, should, and do argue such matters.

To treat a poem's thematic meaning as its speaker's realization requires us to understand it as a personal or particular appraisal of particular experience. In this matter poets may be seen to attend subjects of human interest with characteristic human regard; evaluation in poetry as a whole, exhibiting wide variety in explicitness and subtlety of appraisal, covers a wide range of situations involving one self with other persons and external objects. Copious documentation of variety in evaluation within poems exists already in critical exegeses in poetry textbooks and other sources. Still it will be useful, in considering meanings of poems as the realizations by their speakers of significances, to recall something of the large limits within which such appraisals range.

Toward one end of the spectrum of possibilities, an appraisive conclusion may lay claim to realization of a universal truth, which may be stated in the poem rather abstractly, as of assured relevance to human conduct generally. Thus Milton, in "On His Blindness," submits the question of his irksome disability to "Patience," from whom he learns God's attitude toward the human condition:

> When I consider how my light is spent
> Ere half my days in this dark world and wide,
> And that one talent which is death to hide
> Lodged with me useless, though my soul more bent
> To serve therewith my Maker, and present
> My true account, lest he returning chide,
> "Doth God exact day-labor, light denied?"

I fondly ask. But Patience, to prevent
That murmur, soon replies, "God doth not need
Either man's work or his own gifts. Who best
Bear his mild yoke, they serve Him best. His state
Is kingly: thousands at his bidding speed,
And post o'er land and ocean without rest;
They also serve who only stand and wait."

Doubtless this poem could return us profitably to the biographical question. We know of course that, far from being a blessedly patient man, Milton was a restless old tiger whose idea of standing and waiting was to stamp one foot after the other. Nor does the gnashing Milton altogether release his grip on this poem to the piously murmuring speaker who realizes his need for resigned fortitude and its favor in the sight of God. For example, in the poem Patience *says* that God does not need men, but Patience also acknowledges quite a number of them running errands for God, and a terrestrial logic might conclude that they are doing errands because the errands are needed.

I am not hinting at ambiguities which Milton intends, for the speaker of the piece as we have it is surely a faithfully enduring projection from Milton's very own person, seeking to accept his fate without whining or recrimination, in assurance of God's grace. But in so far as Milton wrote his poem in search of solid ground for resignation which his speaker does not precisely locate, I may point toward some element of failure in the poet's vision. Even if I am right, the poem may be the more touching for being something less than a perfect comfort for a wearing personal problem.

Whether or not the speaker's realization is unsettled, plainly it is his recognition of the relevance to him of generally applicable spiritual law. That readers have found personally relevant Milton's realization of living force in one of the eternal verities, as his speaker discerns it, need hardly be stressed. Indeed, the last line of the piece has almost been rubbed smooth of associations with its immediate poetic context by frequent quotation as a general maxim for human belief and right conduct.

If in one poem a speaker's realization may be of the personal relevance of an established truth or well-known point of doctrine, in still another poem an appraisive conclusion may include no more public a case than is implicit in the personal, subjective impact of a realization. We note the effect in Emily Dickinson's "Because I Could Not Stop for Death," in which death is figured as a gentleman caller who drives the speaker out in his carriage to her new and unexpected permanent address, marked by her own gravesite. She tells the story thus:

> Because I could not stop for Death,
> He kindly stopped for me;
> The carriage held but just ourselves
> And Immortality.

> We slowly drove, he knew no haste,
> And I had put away
> My labor, and my leisure too,
> For his civility.

> We passed the school where children played
> At wrestling in a ring;
> We passed the fields of gazing grain,
> We passed the setting sun.

> We paused before a house that seemed
> A swelling of the ground;
> The roof was scarcely visible,
> The cornice but a mound.

> Since then 'tis centuries; but each
> Feels shorter than the day
> I first surmised the horses' heads
> Were toward eternity.

The experience represented in the poem is its speaker's change or even reversal of awareness. Thoroughly involved in human affairs, she comes to realize, during the course of her narrated experience, that hers is an eternal destiny. Implicit in her realization is a reflexive appraisive conclusion; it was an enormous realization. It somehow changes everything— her sense of her interests, her nature, time; a real metamorphosis in her sense of the nature of her engagement in experience. Nothing that has happened to her in the numberless centuries since her moment of realization is as remarkable or as memorable as the realization itself. That was her moment of unpredicable awe. Did the moment fill her with gladness, fear, expectation, dread, or even regret? It is not part of her appraisive conclusion to tell us, for the inescapable fact of limitless implication which she discovers, or realizes, renders irrelevant any limited human response.

To treat the poem's meaning as its speaker's realization of significance—whether that realization leads, as in the Milton poem, to a general proposition about life or whether, as in Emily Dickinson's poem, its effect is to leave the speaker speechless—is to consider the poem as a piece of discourse representing an act of conscious recognition or awareness. Thus, dramatic theory encourages us to think of poetry as designative discourse, in which what a speaker comes to think about the character of his object of interest in the poem stands at the center of our regard for what he means in saying his poem.

It is some such consideration of the poem as a report of awareness that has led to modern doctrines of poetry as a form of knowledge. To be aware of something is in some sense to know it; to become aware, or to become more fully aware, of something is somehow to learn or know more. Some part of modern speculation concerning poetic knowledge, involving invidious comparison between the better or fuller or higher knowledge of poetry and the lesser knowledge of science, doubtless rests on a mystique proceeding in a direct line of descent from Henri Bergson's metaphysics to T. E. Hulme's aesthetics to Allen Tate's theory of poetry as knowledge.[12] As Tate puts the theoretic conclusion, "It is my contention . . . that the high forms of literature offer us the only complete, and thus the most responsible versions of our experience." Tate states the mystique to which he refers his contention as follows: "The point of view . . . is influenced by the late . . . T. E. Hulme. . . . It is the belief, philosophically tenable, in a radical discontinuity between the physical and spiritual realms." [13] I believe that Tate means by saying that this view is philosophically tenable only that it is subject neither to proof nor disproof; and whether or not its implication would land poetry somewhere among the orders of possible mystical intuitions of reality is for us, in the context of my present discussion, a consideration of dubious relevance. More certainly relevant is the immediate problem addressed by Tate's conclusion. Whatever else may be said of his contention, it reflects a widely felt sense of distress concerning the impact of science on human values, including claims which reasonably can be made for poetry as representation of reality. As Tate puts the vexing cause of his particular case for poetry as knowledge, "On the one hand, we assume that all experience can be ordered scientifically, an assumption that we are almost ready to confess has intensified if it has not actually created our distress; but on the other hand, this assumption has logically reduced the spiritual realm to irresponsible emotion, to what the positivists of our time see as irrelevant feeling; it is irrelevant because it cannot be reduced to the terms of positivist procedure." [14]

Although the denial of cognitive function to poetry to which Tate refers expresses one dimension of modern logical posi-

---

[12] I have discussed this line of influence at some length in "Modern Literary Thought: The Consciousness of Abstracting," *Speech Monographs,* XX, (March, 1953). See especially 1–3, 12–16.

[13] Allen Tate, *On the Limits of Poetry* (New York: The Swallow Press and William Morrow and Co., 1948), 4.

[14] *Ibid.*

tivism, the denial is of course by no means a recent one. I neither can nor wish to pretend to explain theory of knowledge since the late eighteenth century, but we are well aware of the attention devoted in this body of theory to subjective factors involved in perception. Hence, as we know, the view of poetry as merely subjective response or pure creation has found ready support in epistemological analysis reserving to science the discovery of verifiable knowledge.[15] But, as this sort of analysis is not merely a recent one, neither is it merely a recent effort by some poetic theorists to exhibit poetry as publicly significant designation, that is to say, as denotative or meaningful discourse.

In the earliest phases of what we have taught ourselves to call the Romantic movement, the generous mind of Coleridge conceived a sweeping plan for reconciliation between the Aristotelian belief that the poet is a discoverer of some part of the workings of suprasensible reality and the belief, waxing in Coleridge's time and which of course he shared, that the poet is a creator expressing his own unique personality in making his own poetic world. As I understand him, Coleridge located the point of contact between these seemingly incompatible beliefs or ontological doctrines through his identifying suprasensible reality as itself a continuous process of creation by the great I Am or God. Thus, for Coleridge, the poet became god of the poetic world which he created and which was embodied in the particulars of his poem. He created his poetic world not as an act of defiance against that greatest of all poets, the great I Am, author of a universe every part of whose autobiographical epic concluded with "To be continued," but as a human emblem of divine creativity and a proud

15 Of the variety of statements to this effect doubtless that of Richards, distinguishing poetic "pseudo-statement" from scientific "statement" whose "truth is ultimately a matter of verification as this is understood in the laboratory," has most stimulated modern students of poetics to reflection and discussion. See I. A. Richards, "Poetry and Belief," in Robert Wooster Stallman (ed.), *Critiques and Essays in Criticism, 1920–1948* (New York: Ronald Press Co., 1949), especially p. 329.

legatee, through his inheritance of the fertile Secondary Imagination, of some portion of the universal shaping power.[16]

Doubtless the stress of Coleridge's reconciliation fell on the poet as creator rather than discoverer, and in any event, as we have noted, Romantic thought generally drifted away from treatment of the poet as discoverer of truth, of poetry as cognitive discourse.

I do not know what reconciliation between treatment of the poet as both subjective creator and objective discoverer finally will be effected by further consideration of poetry in the perspective of dramatic theory. But dramatic theory implies that theoretic reconciliation of these views is desirable, for its convincing formulation would be but the rational case for expectancies which are stimulated by dramatic doctrine and

[16] Admittedly, Coleridge's theory of poetry, amid, and sometimes by implication as part of, autobiographical anecdotes in his *Biographia Literaria,* is something of a literary stew, if a rich one; and I do not insist that his ideas are reducible to the simple recipe offered here. Nor will merely a few citations certify this interpretation. But a full argument for this view of Coleridge's opinions would surely include among pivotal passages—see Stauffer (ed.), *Selected Poetry and Prose of Coleridge*—these: "This principle ['a truth self-grounded, unconditional and known by its own light'—p. 247], and so characterized, manifests itself in the *sum* or *I Am;* which I shall hereafter indiscriminately express by the words spirit, self, and self-consciousness" (p. 248); ". . . if we elevate our conception to the absolute self, the great eternal *I Am,* then the principle of being, and of knowledge, of idea, and of reality, the ground of existence, and the ground of the knowledge of existence, are absolutely identical . . ." (p. 249); "The *Imagination* then, I consider either as primary, or secondary. The primary *Imagination* I hold to be the living Power and prime Agent of all human Perception, and as a repetition in the finite mind of the eternal act of creation in the infinite *I Am.* The secondary Imagination I consider as an echo of the former, co-existing with the conscious will, yet still as identical with the primary in the *kind* of its agency, and differing only in *degree,* and in the *mode* of its operation. It dissolves, diffuses, dissipates, in order to re-create; or where this process is rendered impossible, yet still at all events it struggles to idealize and to unify. It is essentially *vital,* even as all objects (as objects) are essentially fixed and dead" (p. 263); "What is poetry? is so nearly the same question with, what is a poet? that the answer to the one is involved in the solution to the other. For it is a distinction resulting from the poetic genius itself, which sustains and modifies the images, thoughts, and emotions of the poet's own mind" (p. 268).

which are extremely widespread, if not universal, among the readers of poetry. Simply, most of us expect expression of the poet's personal vision in his poems, thus identifying the subjectivity of his utterance. But we also expect from that utterance insight into more than the poet's own psyche, as one more psychological case study; we expect insight into conditions of and possibilities for human existence.

Treating the poem's meaning as a speaker's realization of significance does not mean that we are required to expect from poems incontrovertible new truths, although of course if we ever do receive an incontrovertible truth from a poem, I am sure we should feel free to keep it. But dramatic doctrine does imply that we may expect from the poem appraisals of selected aspects of experience deriving from the poet's personal perspective which, in reading his poem, we may make our own.

Such a view does not reduce the poem to its author's personality, but it does account for the fact that the poem is not possible without a particular poet's having written it. Richard Ellmann, calling Yeats's poem "The Tower" a mighty work, states that it seems to have the weight of Yeats's whole life behind it. [17] I do not cite Ellmann's as a particular critical judgment with which I happen to agree but as an example, of the most illustrious sort, of what many generations of readers have come to expect from poems. We expect them to convey the weight, or some part of the weight, of their authors' lives. His or her poems will tell us the kind of person their author is—what he values, what he dispraises, how he looks at things. Let me be grand: We expect to hear rumors in the poem of its author's existential commitment.

He or she, he-or-she-himself-or-herself-I:—that is the informing voice we hunger to hear in the poem. Of course we attach a self-respecting condition to our hunger, for, as E. E. Cummings' Olaf would have said, there are some pieces we

[17] Ellman, *Yeats: The Man and the Masks*, 250.

will not eat. Nothing raggedy-taggedy for us, who want to hear the speakers of poems utter poems rather than just shout at us. But, when an author informs the mob of words in the dictionary with telling and precise order, their master's voice shall be heard.

It has sometimes interested me to think what might have happened in theory and practice of poetry over the past forty or so years if Eliot had flatly and unambiguously announced that the poem is simply an objective correlative of its author's consciousness or awareness of his own life or some phase of his own life's experience. But of course it is an unreal question. There is a time, as Marx and Ecclesiastes have pointed out, for all things, and the time was not ripe in Eliot's critically influential but embattled early period for announcement in terms like these of the objective correlative. He had all those Georgian poets on his hands, with their slumped interpretation of Romantic doctrine. Hence, we praise him for a polemic admirably designed for its occasion. With Hulme, Pound, and others he sought to restore vigor to poetry in English which even dogs and cats could read, as Marianne Moore said in another context of some kinds of verse. But, in strenuously urging impersonality against expressionism, some part of Eliot's speculations led us, in contemplating the poem's nature, not into the light of the rose garden but simply down the garden path. The poem is not, as in part Eliot encouraged us to believe it is, the place in which the poet loses himself but one in which he finds himself. Doubtless the encounter is not invariably pleasant.

If my comments, even so near the conclusion of my remarks, become themselves almost a polemic, it is that of a man who insists on camping with his enemies. In tracing history of ideas, we are disappointed in a man who finishes the thought he starts, as a thinker who didn't have much to start up anyhow. But Eliot and other impersonalist critics started lines of modern inquiry of continuing moment. The impersonalist puzzled, as the dramatic theorist still puzzles, the crucial relation between the poem's and the poet's being, between poem's meaning and poet's life and outlook. The impersonal theorist's emphasis on the poet as maker set some part of the terms, not for the dramatic solution, but for dramatic theory's more inclusive consideration of the poet as both expressionist and maker. We may hear in the poem, as the Romantics warned us that we would hear, its author's voice enunciating the quality of his being. But the voice is clear only to the extent that it makes not a noise but a poem. Indeed, we may think, the measure of the poem's making will be the measure of just how clear the poet's voice has become. When, as readers, we have heard that informed and informing voice, we will have understood the poem; when, as oral interpreters, we project that voice, we will have helped other readers understand the poem, or understand it more richly.

Or so I think.